This book must be returned by the date specified at the time of issue as
the DATE DUE FOR RETURN.
The loan may be extended (personally, by post, telephone or online) for
a further period if the book is not required by another reader, by quoting
the above number / author / title.

Enquiries: 01709 336774
www.rotherham.gov.uk/libraries

BRITISH
WILDLIFE

First published in 2010 by Miles Kelly Publishing Ltd
Harding's Barn, Bardfield End Green, Thaxted, Essex, CM6 3PX, UK

Copyright © Miles Kelly Publishing Ltd 2010

2 4 6 8 10 9 7 5 3 1

Editorial Director Belinda Gallagher
Art Director Jo Brewer
Project Editor Amanda Askew
Cover Designer Simon Lee
Designers Jo Brewer, Michelle Canatella, Rick Caylor
Image Manager Liberty Newton
Indexer Marie Lorimer
Production Manager Elizabeth Collins
Reprographics Stephan Davis, Jennifer Hunt, Ian Paulyn

Miles Kelly would like to thank The Wildlife Trusts
for their valuable contribution to this book.

ISBN 978-1-84810-337-5

Printed in China

British Library Cataloguing-in-Publication Data
A catalogue record for this book is available
from the British Library

Made with paper from a sustainable forest

www.mileskelly.net
info@mileskelly.net

www.factsforprojects.com

Self-publish your
children's book

buddingpress.co.uk

ACKNOWLEDGEMENTS
Artwork is from the Miles Kelly Artwork Bank

The publishers would like to thank the
following sources for the use of their
photographs:

ardea.com Cover Duncan Usher

Ben Osborne 384

Bob Langrish 83

Colin Varndell 322(r); 325(r); 328(r); 329(r);
330(r); 332(r); (r); 351(r); 355(r); 357(r); 361(r)

Dennis McGuire 42(tl), 42(tr)

Still Pictures 340(r) D.Harms/WILDLIFE

Dreamstime.com 12(tr) Jscalev, 31(tl) J Handt

Fotolia.com 12(tl) Brian Lambert; 15(t) Jeremy
Turner, (bl) Dave Timms; 17(tl) vchphoto,
(tr) Steve Mutch, (bl); 18(bl) Canon_Bob,
(tr) Van Truan, (br) sumnersgraphicsinc;
19(l) Anette Linnea Rasmussen, (r) Paul
Murphy; 20(b) Becky Stares; 21(br) Regis
Gontier; 22(tr) John Barber; 23(b) bluefern;
24(b) Paul Murphy; 25(t) DE Photography,
(bl) Geza Farkas, (br) Yuri Timofeyev;
26(t) MichaelJordan, (br) Detlef Rother;
27(b) Anette Linnea Rasmusse; 28(tr) Otmar
Smit, (bl) Anyka, (br) Saoirse Mac Cárthaigh;
29(tl), (tr) Jerome Ferron; 30(tl) Bobo Ling,
(tr) Darryl Sleath; 31(tl) Gunta Klavina,
(tr) Michel Gatti, (b) Sally Wallis; 32–33 Oleg
Belyakov; 34(tr) Elenathewise, (br) Andrzej
Tokarski; 35(tr); 36(tl) Marilyn Barbone,
(b) Tomasz Kubis; 37 Phil King; 38(t) Graeme,
(b) vchphoto; 39 photogirl11; 40(l) Bine,
(r) Kolja Pedersen; 42(b) Eric Weight;
43(t) JMPIC, (r) Candida Godson, (b) Robert
Ford; 44(tr) Tony, (b) Anne Katrin Figge;
216–217 MLA Photography; 322(c) AndreyTTL;
336(c) Robyn Mackenzie; 353(c) Olena
Kucherenko

FLPA 348(c) Roger Wilmshurst

iStockphoto.com 10–11 Angus Forbes;
13(t) AtWaG; 14(r) Klaas Lingbeek-van Kranen;
15(br) Andrew Howe; 16(r) Chris Crafter;
17(br) Karel Broz; 20(t) Tommounsey;
21(tl) erikfred, 22(br) Giorgio Perbellini;
23(t) creacart; 26(bl) Kurt Hahn; 30(b) Jerome
Whittingham; 35(br) Jerome Whittingham;
36(tr) John Anderson; 44(tl) Andrew Howe;
46–47 Ken Canning; 84–85 Charlie Bishop;
198–199 Giorgio Perbellini; 208–209 Len Tillim

Richard Burkmar 39, 42

WTPL 45

All other photographs are from:
Corel, digitalvision, Image State, PhotoDisc

CONTENTS

AMPHIBIANS & REPTILES 198-207

FRESHWATER FISH 208-215

MINIBEASTS 216-269

WILDFLOWERS 270–317

Organized by colour

TREES & SHRUBS
318–371

Organized by leaf shape

BRITISH WILDLIFE

Animals that have lived in Britain for thousands of years are **described as being 'native'.** Some of our native animals are so common, you will probably already be familiar with them.

BLACKBIRD

With their black plumage (feathers) and yellow bills, male blackbirds are easy to identify. However, females are much harder to recognize because they are brown all over, with a speckled breast. Blackbirds hop through leaf litter searching for insects, berries and worms to eat. *See page 168.*

Blackbirds are familiar garden birds, but they can also be spotted in woodland and farmland.

WOODLOUSE

These minibeasts are among the easiest to find, especially in woodland and garden habitats. Despite their appearance, these animals are crustaceans, not insects. This means they are more closely related to crabs than beetles! *See page 222.*

Pill woodlice are able to roll into a ball if they are disturbed.

MALLARD

The most common ducks in the world, mallards live not only in Britain but throughout Europe, Asia, Africa and North America. Males, which are called drakes, have bottle-green heads and black, grey and white bodies. In summer, they lose this bright colouring and take on the same dull brown plumage as females. Mallards are usually tame and approach people for food. *See page 99.*

Mallards are very adaptable and can live in almost all types of aquatic habitat.

DARTMOOR PONY

In some of Britain's wilder places ponies roam free. Dartmoor, Exmoor, Shetland and New Forest ponies are all examples of these hardy animals, which are able to survive in harsh habitats. *See page 83.*

Dartmoor ponies have long, thick fur and manes to protect them from the cold.

COMMON WASP

If you spot many common wasps in one place, you could be near a nest. These stinging insects live in large groups of up to 1000 individuals, and they build their nests in old burrows, garden sheds or house lofts. If in danger, wasps can produce a special chemical called a pheromone, which attracts other wasps to come to their aid. *See page 232.*

Wasps build their nests using a papery pulp that they produce by chewing up wood. Wasp larvae develop in the hexagonal cells in the nest.

SONG THRUSH

These birds look similar to mistle thrushes but they are smaller and have slightly darker colouring. Song thrushes often dash or rush across the ground, head leaning over to one side, as they listen for insects. Their loud song can often be heard at dusk. *See page 164.*

WOODPIGEON

Large, grey, stout-bodied birds, woodpigeons are common in parks, gardens, woodlands and farmland. They waddle when they walk and are able to eat all sorts of food. The pigeons that are found in towns are likely to be descended from rock doves (feral pigeons) which are smaller than woodpigeons. *See page 142.*

ANIMALS FROM ABROAD

Britain has only been an island for about 8000 years. Before then, animals roamed freely across a large landmass, which included Britain. Since then, British wildlife has been largely cut off from Europe. However, people have introduced new species, or types, of animal to Britain, many of which have settled and established populations. These animals are called non-native species.

PARAKEET

Parrots and parakeets mostly live in hot, tropical countries. However, an increasingly large number of green parakeets now live wild in southeast England. The birds were probably pets that escaped or were set free and they have adapted well to the cooler British climate.

Only male green parakeets have a pink collar and black facial markings.

MUNTJAC

Small deer from Asia, muntjacs were brought to Britain about 100 years ago. A number of them escaped from the wildlife park where they lived and successful groups of muntjacs have since become established.

MINK

American minks have escaped from fur farms in Britain and now live wild in the countryside. These mammals threaten water vole populations in the areas where they live and are considered to be pests.

RED-NECKED WALLABY

These animals come from Tasmania, a small island off Australia. They were brought to British zoos and parks but those that escaped have bred in the wild. There have been populations in Scotland, Sussex and the Peak District.

The red-necked wallaby is one of the largest wallabies, so it can easily be mistaken for a kangaroo.

RED-EARED TERRAPIN

Terrapins are a type of reptile. The red-eared terrapin is an American species that has become established in Britain. Originally kept as pets, these animals can grow quite large and give a nasty bite, so many have been released into the wild. Unfortunately, they attack and eat ducklings.

The red-eared terrapin can easily be identified by the red stripe behind its ears. It is fond of basking in the sunshine.

GREY SQUIRREL

These small mammals were first introduced to Britain from the USA around 100 years ago, and they have settled over large parts of the country. Sadly, grey squirrels have forced the native red squirrel out of most of its natural habitat. *See page 67.*

Squirrels scurry about in trees or on the ground, looking for food such as nuts.

COMMON PHEASANT

These long-tailed, brightly coloured birds originally came from Asia, and they have been living in Britain for hundreds of years. They were brought here as game birds and are still bred and released for sport. *See page 109.*

An adult male pheasant is unmistakable with its green head, red eye patch and long tail.

NATIONAL PARKS

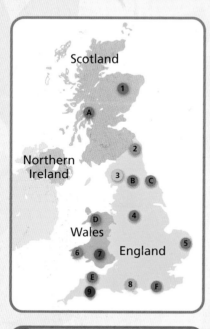

Scotland

Northern Ireland

Wales

England

There are more than 6000 National Parks in the world, covering about 12 percent of the Earth's surface, and 15 of them are in England, Wales and Scotland. Outside National Parks, organizations like The Wildlife Trusts manage nature reserves where wildlife is given special protection.

A Loch Lomond and the Trossachs
B Yorkshire Dales
C North Yorkshire Moors
D Snowdonia
E Exmoor
F South Downs

---

2 Northumberland, northern England
The hills and valleys of Northumberland are good places to spy insects, birds and mammals. Emperor moths, peacock butterflies, martins, swallows, cuckoos and badgers can be found here.

Badger, page 72

---

1 Cairngorms, Scotland
Mountains, forests, rivers and lochs provide plenty of interesting habitats in the Cairngorms. Look out for red deer, sika deer, reindeer, red squirrels and birds of prey, especially ospreys and falcons.

Peregrine falcon, page 108

---

3 Lake District, northwest England
Britain's largest national park, the Lake District provides a range of habitats. Look out for red squirrels, ospreys, pipistrelle bats, toads and the high brown fritillary butterfly, which lives in the Cumbrian Low Fells.

4 Peak District, Midlands

With heather moors, woodlands, bogs, rivers and cliffs, the Peak District has many habitats. Wildlife includes polecats, water shrews and water voles, although water voles are becoming increasingly rare.

Polecat, page 75

5 The Broads, Norfolk, eastern England

Huge areas of wetland in this park make it a good place in which to spot wildlife that prefers to live in damp habitats. Frogs, dragonflies, herons, mallards, kingfishers and newts may be seen.

Kingfisher, page 150

6 Pembrokeshire Coast, Wales

The only entirely coastal national park, the Pembrokeshire Coast is a good place to find water and coastal birds. You can also look out for seals, porpoises, dolphins and even whales or basking sharks.

7 Brecon Beacons, Wales

A mountainous park with spectacular scenery, the Brecon Beacons are a good place to spot lapwings, otters, water voles and great crested newts.

Otter, page 73

8 New Forest, southern England

Rare types of animal found here include the sand lizard, New Forest cicada and the stag beetle. It is a good place to find lizards and snakes.

Stag beetle, page 249

9 Dartmoor, southwest England

The largest and wildest open space in southern England, Dartmoor is home to a huge variety of wildlife, such as swifts, swallows, field voles, common lizards and hedgehogs.

WATCHING WILDLIFE

The British countryside, woodlands, parks and gardens, are home to many different animals. Some of our wildlife is easy to spot and some is much more difficult. There are useful pieces of equipment that may help you to find many of the animals listed in this book, and a few handy hints to set you safely on your way.

USEFUL TOOLS

Binoculars
It is almost impossible to get close enough to birds to get a good look at the shape of their bills or the colour of their legs. A pair of binoculars magnifies things and makes them appear larger, so identification becomes much easier.

Magnifying glass
Many invertebrates, such as ants and bugs, are too small to see clearly with the naked eye. A magnifying glass allows you to see their limbs, antennae and other interesting details.

Small containers
Old shells, feathers and other interesting specimens can be kept in containers and taken home for further examination. Never take anything alive home or disturb an animal's habitat.

Ants, page 230

Notebook and pencil
Record notes and make sketches in a notebook. Sketching an animal makes you look closely at its features, which will help with identification. Taking photographs is another useful way of keeping records.

HANDY HINTS

When you go out in search of wildlife you should follow these simple rules:

1 Shut gates after you, or farm animals may escape and come to harm.
2 Keep dogs under close control because they scare other animals away.
3 Stay on or near paths so you don't stray onto other people's land or get lost.
4 Do not pick plants, but you can collect some leaves.
5 Respect the animals' habitats or homes.

Blue tit, page 176

Keep quiet

Most animals fear being caught, and so they react quickly to the slightest sound. Unless you are looking for wildlife in silence, many animals will have disappeared from view long before you get close to them.

Stay safe

If you are exploring a new area take a map with you and plan a route. It is always a good idea to take food and water. Never venture out without telling an adult where you are going and when you plan to return.

Use your ears

Occasionally just stand or sit still and listen. You may hear all sorts of interesting wildlife noises. If you stay in one place for long enough, some animals may come up to investigate you!

Look and look again

Most animals are hidden from view, so try peering inside hedgerows, lifting up leaves and raising logs and rocks to see what may be lurking underneath. Always remember to put things back the way you found them. Never look in a birds' nest while it is in use.

Wood mouse, page 59

IDENTIFYING VERTEBRATES

Scientists group animals according to their characteristics, such as the number of legs they have. This helps to identify animals and work out how they are related to one another. The most important characteristic of verebrates is that they have a backbone. They also have a brain and a complex nervous system.

AMPHIBIANS

Amphibians lay their eggs in water and many of them need to live in or near a damp habitat to survive. They have moist skin that can absorb oxygen, and in some cases produces toxins, or poisons, to protect the animal from predators. The young often look very different to the adult, for example, tadpoles, which are young frogs.

This tadpole has hatched from an egg and is able to swim. It will grow into an adult frog. See page 200.

REPTILES

Reptiles have scaly bodies. Their young hatch from eggs, which are laid on land. They cannot control their body temperature and hibernate when it is cold or bask in the sun.

Although slow worms look like snakes, they are actually legless lizards. See page 206.

BIRDS

Birds are vertebrates that have feathers and bills (beaks). Their hind limbs are adapted for perching. Their front limbs are wings and most birds can fly. Young birds hatch from eggs.

Robins are highly territorial. They are usually seen alone or in pairs during spring and summer. See page 162.

MAMMALS

Mammals are vertebrates that have fur, or hair, and they feed their young with milk. The young are born, not hatched from eggs. Mammals are able to control their body temperature, which means they can survive in cold places. Most mammals have four limbs, although in bats, the forelimbs are wings. The smallest wild British mammals are shrews, mice and bats.

Fallow deer live in wooded areas, as part of a medium-sized herd. See page 82.

FISH

Fish are water-living vertebrates with bodies that are adapted for their habitat. Most fish have torpedo-shaped bodies that can move easily through the water. They breathe using special organs called gills, which absorb oxygen from the water. Most fish have scales on their bodies.

Some fish are especially adaptable, such as the brown trout, which lives in both fresh water and the sea. See page 210.

IDENTIFYING INVERTEBRATES

More than 90 percent of all living animals are invertebrates – creatures without backbones. This group includes arthropods such as insects, annelids such as worms and molluscs such as snails.

ARTHROPODS

Arthropods are invertebrates with bodies that are protected by a hard outer skin, called an exoskeleton. Their bodies are usually divided into segments. There are four main groups of arthropods:
- Insects
- Crustaceans
- Spiders
- Millipedes and centipedes

INSECTS

Insects have bodies that are divided into three segments: the head, the thorax and the abdomen. Three pairs of legs are attached to the thorax, and, if there are any, wings too. The heads have the sensory organs such as eyes and antennae.

The hard outer wings of the ladybird protect the soft, flying wings underneath. See page 247.

CRUSTACEANS

Crustaceans have two pairs of antennae and eyes on stalks. Most crustaceans live in water and breathe through gills, but some, such as woodlice, live on land.

MILLIPEDES & CENTIPEDES

Millipedes and centipedes are arthropods that live on land and have many pairs of legs. Each body segment has either one pair of legs (centipedes) or two (millipedes).

Centipedes catch prey with their claws. See page 266.

SPIDERS

Spiders' bodies have two main segments and four pairs of legs. Spiders often have more than two eyes and can produce silk from their abdomens to make their webs.

Wasp spiders spin webs to catch their prey. See page 269.

ANNELIDS

Annelids are worms, such as the earthworm, with bodies that are divided into segments. Each segment contains a complete set of organs. Most worms are burrowers.

Earthworms spend most of their time underground. However, they come to the surface at night and in wet weather. See page 218.

MOLLUSCS

Molluscs include octopuses, squids, garden snails, slugs and shelled sea creatures. These animals have soft bodies and no skeleton. Their soft body may be protected by a hard shell. Snails and slugs have rough 'tongues' and a 'foot'. This part of their body is used for movement.

Snails eat plants using their rough mouthpart, called a radula, which scrapes food, tearing it into tiny pieces. See page 221.

WILDLIFE IN SPRING

Spring is a time when days get longer and most things begin to grow. At the beginning of spring there is little sign of new life, except for the closed buds on trees and the first snowdrops. By the end of spring, the countryside is green and busy with new life.

BLOSSOMING TREES

Some trees burst into blossom in spring, even before leaves have broken out of their buds. Insects emerge from hibernation, or from their eggs or pupae, to drink the sweet nectar.

Blossom is the name given to the flowers of some trees, especially fruit trees. They are either pink or white. See page 321.

EARLY FLOWERS

With a ready-made store of food, flowering bulbs, such as primrose and wood anemones, start to produce shoots early in spring, long before other flowers bloom.

Primrose flowering is one of the sure signs of spring. See page 313.

SNAKES & LIZARDS

Reptiles need the warm weather of spring to become active. By April and May, lizards and snakes are more visible than earlier in the year. They can often be seen basking in the heat of the sun on rocks or stones.

Adders are Britain's only venomous snake, but they are not aggressive. See page 204.

FROGSPAWN

The first signs of amphibian life appear when frogs mate and lay their eggs, or spawn, in ponds. The spawn is a jelly-like mass, with hundreds of small black spots – the developing tadpoles. Toads usually mate later in spring than frogs. *See pages 200–201.*

Frogspawn can be seen in abundance in garden ponds and other areas of water.

BUTTERFLIES EMERGE

When the days are warm enough butterflies emerge, from their pupae or after hibernating. The peacock butterfly, which has false eyes on its wings, is one of the earliest seen in spring. *See page 256.*

While inside its pupa, a caterpillar transforms into a beautiful butterfly.

SONGBIRDS

In spring songbirds, such as robins and nightingales, begin to prepare their nests for breeding. Some birds can be seen collecting nesting materials, such as leaves and feathers.

Nightingales have an impressive, melodious song. See page 163.

WILDLIFE IN SUMMER

Spring soon turns into summer, and it is difficult to say when one ends and the other begins. During summer, the countryside is a busy place – flowers and trees bloom, and animals born in spring are now active, especially because food is in plentiful supply.

HAWTHORN HABITAT

Between late spring and early summer, hawthorn bushes and trees come into flower, shortly after the leaves have appeared. The prickly stems make a perfect place for birds to nest, protecting the chicks from predators. The common name for hawthorn is May. *See page 353.*

Hawthorn blossom attracts nectar-drinking insects, such as bees. See page 231.

HEDGEHOG MATING

Hedgehogs begin their mating season in summer. Hedgehog courtship can be very noisy and their mating calls can sound quite alarming. *See page 48.*

A male approaches a female, making a snorting noise to show that he wants to mate with her.

FEEDING ON FRUIT

During summer and autumn, edible fruits, such as apples, blackberries and pears, begin to ripen. Some fruits fall from trees long before they are ripe, and are quickly eaten by small mammals and insects.

Mice use their sharp teeth to eat fallen fruits, such as apples. See page 58.

PLAYFUL CUBS

By June, red fox cubs are brave enough to venture out of their den to play. Their mother will be nearby, resting in the shade, watching her young. *See page 71.*

Red foxes life in family groups in dens, which they dig into the earth or take over from other animals, such as badgers.

FLOWERS BLOOM

In summer, flowers, from roses to foxgloves, burst open to show their range of colours and perfumes. Flowerbeds and pots are in full bloom and in the countryside, you can see fields of red poppies. Insects are attracted to areas with lots of flowers as they feed on nectar.

Poppies can be found singularly or in large groups. See page 296.

INSECTS EVERYWHERE

Butterflies are seen mating, drinking nectar from flowers and resting in the sun. Beetles scurry across soil and, at dusk, moths fly near windows, attracted to the light. Vegetables grow well and they attract insects such as aphids and caterpillars.

Peacock butterflies feed on fragrant buddleia, as well as dandelions, willows and clover. See page 256.

WILDLIFE IN AUTUMN

By September, the heat of summer has been replaced by a cool evening chill. The days are noticeably shorter, and mornings may be misty as often as they are bright. Growth slows down as animals and plants prepare themselves for the winter ahead.

BIRDS FLY AWAY

The shorter days of autumn indicate to birds that it is time to move elsewhere. Many birds that migrate to warmer countries for winter begin to gather for their journey.

Swallows flock together on telephone lines, and prepare for their long journey ahead. See page 156.

ORB WEAVERS

Spiders are busy throughout the year, but autumn is a good time to see their webs in full glory, as morning dew or mist hangs on the fine silk. Many creatures, such as flies, get caught in the threads. *See pages 267–269.*

No two spider webs are ever the same.

CRANE FLIES

These long-legged insects, also known as daddy-long-legs, emerge in September and huge numbers can be seen in gardens and parks.

Adult crane flies have short lives. They are preyed upon by birds, but can shed legs if they get caught. See page 237.

BERRIES & FRUIT

By the end of summer, most fruits and berries have grown fat and juicy. They ripen and fall to the ground during autumn, where they rot or are eaten. Berries that stay on bushes until winter are eaten by birds because their other food sources have become scarce.

Blackberries ripen between July and November depending on the weather.
See page 359.

NUTS RIPEN

Some trees produce nuts, which ripen in autumn. Many creatures take advantage of this new food supply, especially as flowers and fruits begin to die. Squirrels scurry up and down trees, collecting nuts to store. They dig holes in the ground and bury the nuts so they can eat them later in the year.

Acorns are the fruits of oak trees.
See pages 345 and 347.

FALLING LEAVES

Autumn is the time when trees lose their leaves and become stark skeletons against the skyline. This is a good time to watch birds, as there are no leaves for them to hide behind. Tawny owls can sometimes be spotted at dusk as they prepare for night-time hunting. Fungus grows on forest floors.

Trees drop their leaves in preparation for winter.

WILDLIFE IN WINTER

Winter may appear to be a quiet season. Although it appears to be a time for rest and recovery, there is still a lot of activity. Some animals hibernate or migrate to avoid the coldest weather, but others remain active, trying to survive by finding new food sources.

SNOWTRAILS

On snowy mornings, trails left in the snow can reveal what wildlife is still in the garden. Footprints left by birds (shown below), foxes, feral cats, rabbits, field voles and mice can all be identified.

When the ground is covered with snow, birds struggle to find food such as worms.

WINTER COLOUR

Ferns, lichens and mosses all thrive in the damp weather of early winter. They provide splashes of bright colour once the less hardy garden plants have died down. Lichens are sensitive to environmental change and they are used by scientists to study pollution.

Lichens attach themselves to a range or surfaces including walls, trees, rocks and concrete.

IVY FLOWERS

When many plants have died down, ivy is still teeming with life. Ivy produces flowers as late in the year as November. As so few other plants have any nectar, it is a popular place for many insects to visit. *See page 281.*

Red admiral butterflies may be seen drinking from ivy flowers. See page 258.

WINTER FLOCKS

In winter, many birds gather together in groups for warmth and safety. Flocks of tits visit garden bird feeders and starlings gather in their thousands before roosting at night.

Starlings can flock in groups containing thousands of birds. See page 188.

FOX CALLS

During December and January, foxes begin to mate. Females (vixens) produce loud screams to let males know they are ready, and males bark in response. *See page 71.*

After moulting through summer, foxes grow a thick coat to keep them warm in winter.

COMPOSTS

In winter, many invertebrates struggle to survive in such low temperatures. They are also at a higher risk of being eaten by birds as food is scarce. Invertebrates living in compost, however, are protected as the layers insulate them from the cold.

Plant matter in a compost heap decays (rots) over time.

YOUR WILDLIFE GARDEN

You can see wildlife everywhere, including parks, meadows, woodland and even on city streets. One of the best places to discover wildlife is your garden. Gardens are home to many different types of creature, and it is easy to make a garden a welcoming place for many more. Ask an adult if you can help with the gardening, or even have a corner of the garden to look after yourself.

YOU WILL NEED

Young plants, seeds and bulbs
To make a colourful garden that wildlife will want to visit, you'll need plenty of flowers and other plants. You can buy seeds, bulbs and plants at your local garden centre. Flowers that are more open, such as a daisy shape, are more useful for insects.

Watering can
Plants need water to survive. When there is little rain during summer, make sure to water your plants regularly. Collect rainwater in a water butt.

Container
Use an old container to collect your garden waste, such as weeds. Then you can put the waste in a compost heap.

Trowel
A small garden trowel is useful for turning over soil if you plan to search for invertebrates. Wear gardening gloves, too, so you avoid scratches or stings.

MAMMALS

Gardens can attract a range of mammals, from large creatures such as foxes to tiny shrews and mice. Mammals such as hedgehogs will hibernate and forage in piles of leaf litter. Never move leaf litter without first checking if any mammals have made their home there.

NUTS ABOUT NUTS

Hang up a feeder on a tree branch for squirrels to use. Squirrels can help trees to grow because they collect nuts such as acorns and bury them in the garden. *See page 67.*

Squirrels work busily collecting nuts, only carrying one at a time.

LOG PILE

Animals love areas that are undisturbed where they can forage for food. Put a pile of old logs and leaves in a quiet corner of the garden to encourage small mammals and insects.

Small mammals such as field voles are rarely seen because they hide in leaf litter and foliage. See page 63.

MAKE A BAT BOX

Ask an adult to help you nail a box onto a tree for bats to roost in. You can make one, in a similar way to a bird box (see page 37) or buy one from a garden centre. *See pages 53–56.*

The best place to position a bat box is on a tree, high above the ground away from predators.

BIRDS

Although many birds need shrubs and trees to nest in, they will visit small gardens for food. During winter, when food is scarce, seeds and chopped nuts put out on a bird table, or in a bird feeder, will tempt birds. They also need extra food in spring, when adults feed their chicks.

FEEDING FUN

You can buy a bird feeder, seeds and fat balls from your local garden centre. Or, if you want to be creative, fill a yogurt pot with a mixture of solid cooking fat and seeds. Hang it from a tree and birds will soon come to your garden.

Birds such as nuthatches can visit feeders and bird tables. Nuthatches wedge nuts into cracks in trees and hammer them open with their beaks. See page 181.

BATH TIME

Make, or buy, a simple bird bath for birds to drink from and wash themselves in. Make sure there is always plenty of clean water available for them.

Groups of sparrows enjoy bathing and drinking in bird baths. See page 189.

FEATHER THE NEST

Leave out nesting materials, such as feathers and wool, or piles of dead leaves and twigs. In spring, birds will take these materials to build their nests.

This birds' nest has been made from twigs and feathers to keep the eggs and newly hatched chicks warm.

MAKE A BIRD BOX

Finding a place to build a nest is difficult for birds. Putting up a nesting box is a simple way to help birds find a home.

You will need:
- plank of untreated wood, about 1.5 cm x 15 cm x 120 cm
- screws
- screwdriver
- two hinges
- saw
- electric drill with a spade drill bit

Ask an adult to saw and drill the box, and to hang it.

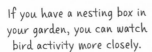
If you have a nesting box in your garden, you can watch bird activity more closely.

1 Plan your box carefully on paper first. Decide how long your sides are going to be, as well as the base and the lid. The lid will need to overhang the box.

2 Cut all your pieces of wood using the saw.

3 Using the drill and spade drill bit, make the hole where the birds will enter the box. Different bird species need different-sized holes.

4 Use the screws to put all the pieces together, except for the lid.

5 Attach the lid with hinges so you can clean the box out.

6 Hang your bird box up high in a tree, where cats cannot reach it.

AMPHIBIANS & REPTILES

These creatures are shy and like plenty of vegetation to hide from predators. Amphibians need water to lay eggs in, and since the young live in water, too, creating a pond attracts them into the garden. Reptiles are rare visitors to most gardens, especially in towns and cities, although grass snakes and slow worms sometimes take refuge in compost piles. Newts, frogs and toads will make their home in a garden pond. If you want to keep pet fish, it's best to make a separate pond for them because fish eat wildlife such as newts and water snails.

THE BIG FREEZE

During winter, frogs and toads will often hibernate at the bottom of a pond. You need to make sure that they get enough oxygen to breathe. Put a tennis ball at the edge of a pond when temperatures drop. You can then take the ball out of the ice, leaving a hole so that oxygen can get through.

Amphibians prefer damp habitats because they breathe through their moist skin.

REPTILE REFUGES

Compost piles can increase the chances of attracting reptiles to a garden. Their dark, warm conditions provide shelter and a habitat. Grass snakes will sometimes lay their eggs in a compost pile. The warmth of the compost helps to incubate the eggs. Slow worms also seek shelter, attracted by the warmth and safety compost piles offer.

Keeping areas of long grass will help to attract reptiles, such as grass snakes, to a garden. See page 205.

BUILD A POND

Ponds encourage wildlife to visit the garden. If you have permission, choose a quiet place in the garden to build a pond. Try to keep it away from trees to avoid falling leaves.

You will need:
• pond liner
• special plants (from most garden centres)
• rocks
• spade
• newspaper, cardboard or old carpet
• plants

Ask an adult to dig the hole and help you build the pond.

Remember that garden ponds need to be fenced off to prevent young children from falling in.

1 Dig a hole about 50 cm x 50 cm x 100 cm. You need at least one side to slope, so frogs and other wildlife can climb in and out.

2 Lay newspaper, card or old carpet and then liner in the hole, leaving extra to go over the edges of the pond.

3 Line the edges with rocks. Fill it with water, then add the plants.

Ponds will attract wildlife to gardens. All ponds need to be looked after, but try to keep plenty of vegetation around the edges as cover for wildlife.

MINIBEASTS

Invertebrates, such as beetles and butterflies, will come into gardens if there are plenty of places for them to live and feed. A good way to do this is to let areas of the garden grow wild. Beetles often like to live in piles of rotting wood, and some butterflies lay their eggs on the underside of nettles and in long grasses.

LIVING IN LITTER

Insects and other invertebrates like to live in leaf litter because the habitat is quiet and undisturbed. Collect dead leaves from the garden and pile them up in a quiet corner. Insects will feel safe and sheltered, away from predators and bad weather conditions.

Millipedes have shiny, cylinder-shaped bodies. They live in leaf litter and climb trees and fences to feed at night. See page 266.

LONG GRASS

Leave some areas of your garden, so the grass grows long. Insects such as leather jackets (crane fly larvae) and caterpillars overwinter in this protected area and new eggs will be laid here in spring.

Caterpillars feed on different kinds of leaves. Some species feed on grasses.

STRAW NESTS

Tie a large handful of drinking straws, plant stems or canes together and place them in a quiet area in the garden. This makes an excellent nesting site for ladybirds and lacewings.

PUDDLE DRINK

Fill a shallow dish or container with small stones. Then add water to make a puddle. Watch butterflies and other insects as they come to drink.

GIVE A BEE A HOME

Bees pollinate flowers, which means that their seeds can develop and grow. You can encourage bees into your garden by growing wildflowers to give them pollen and nectar, and by making a bee home.

You will need:
- open-fronted bird box
- nesting material (such as hamster bedding)
- bamboo
- drill
- glue or string

Ask an adult to drill the holes.

1 Get a bird box and add some nesting material inside.

2 Drill 1-cm-wide holes at the bottom, for bees to use as an entrance.

3 Glue or tie together some bamboo sticks and place in the top hole.

Other nests to make:

Tunnel
Pile up old logs, bricks or a mixture of both and leave plenty of 'tunnel' spaces for bees to crawl into.

Bamboo
Push short pieces of old bamboo into flowerpot holes so bees can get into the hollow centres to lay their eggs.

Flowerpot
Put chicken wire into an old flowerpot and add handfuls of dry moss, or small pet bedding for the bees to use as nesting material.

Bees may lay their eggs inside these bamboo sticks.

FLOWERS

Flowers make pollen and nectar, which attract insects to the garden. The insects then attract birds and mammals. Most flowers and grasses are useful to animals, because they provide food and shelter.

MINI-MEADOW

Meadows are areas where grass and some flowers grow freely. Try leaving a patch of grass to grow long. This gives small creatures, such as insects, mice and shrews, a place to hide from predators.

Long grass and wild areas encourage wildlife to your garden.

NETTLE NESTS

If you can, leave an area of stinging nettles in your garden. Make sure they're in a place where people don't need to walk and never touch them because they sting.

Many butterflies, such as small tortoiseshells, lay their eggs on nettle leaves.

TEASEL SEEDS

Teasels and sunflowers attract wild birds because their seedheads are an important source of food in winter, when most plants have died. Try growing them in your garden during the summer months, and then watch to see which birds visit your garden.

Goldfinch like to feed on the seeds of teasels and thistles. See page 193.

PICK YOUR PLANTS

Different plants and flowers attract different insects. Nectar-giving flowers, for example, will encourage bees to your garden.

Lavender
Honeybees collect pollen and nectar from flowers, which they use to produce honey in their hives. They may visit up to 1000 flowers in one day and they especially like lavender.

Bees use lavender nectar to produce high-quality honey.

Honeysuckle
There are more than 175 types of plants related to honeysuckle in the world. Many are sweet scented and attract a huge range of insects, including bees. When the shrub becomes larger, it also provides a nesting site for birds. *See page 282.*

Honeysuckle is a climbing shrub that spreads quickly. It is often found covering walls and fences.

Buddleia
The butterfly bush, or buddleia, is a magnet to butterflies, particularly the peacock and small tortoiseshell, because the tiny flowers hold sweet-tasting nectar. *See page 342.*

Butterflies feed on the nectar from buddleia flowers.

TREES & SHRUBS

Many creatures need trees, shrubs and plants to survive. They use them for food, shelter and as a place to lay eggs and protect their young from predators. Hawthorn and bramble produce berries. These provide food for birds, which is especially important as winter approaches.

FRUIT TREES

Plant trees, shrubs and other plants with flowers and fruits. Their flowers and fruits attract wildlife to your garden to feed. *See page 321.*

Many birds, such as this female blackbird, rely on fruit to eat, especially during autumn and winter.

SHELTER

Avoid cutting back plants too much, especially trees and shrubs, because they provide vital shelter for animals. Birds nest in the boughs, away from predators, and insects and small mammals use the leaves to hide.

Nests built in trees provide chicks with shelter and protection.

HOLLY

Grow a holly bush in your garden. The distinctive leaves of holly are thick and waxy with spiky edges. The berries, which grow in autumn and winter, attract birds, such as redwings, blackbirds and fieldfares. Holly berries are important during the cold seasons when other food sources are unavailable. *See page 344.*

Holly provides a lot of colour in winter months with deep-green leaves and red berries.

PLANT A TREE

Planting trees is great for the environment and easier than you might think. Make sure you have enough space and choose a native tree, such as oak or apple, where the benefits are even greater because they provide food and shelter for wildlife.

You will need:
• bucket • tree sapling • spade

1 Before planting your sapling, give the roots a good soak in a bucket of water.

2 Carefully remove the sapling from its container. Check it for damage and remove any broken roots.

3 Decide on your planting spot. Dig a hole twice as wide and slightly deeper than the roots.

4 You may need to make the hole bigger to avoid bending the roots – try your sapling in the hole to check.

5 Place your sapling upright in the hole. Break up the dug-out soil and fill in carefully but firmly around the roots.

6 Tread down the soil firmly and add some more soil if needed. Tread down again.

7 Take the pieces of turf saved from earlier and place them upside down around your sapling and press them down.

8 Finally, 'heel in' the earth around the tree. Give your sapling a gentle tug – it should be firmly in place.

9 Tidy up and apply mulch (material laid down to keep in moisture) around the base of your sapling.

HEDGEHOG

These prickly mammals are welcome visitors to gardens, as they eat many pests. Hedgehogs are carnivores and eat slugs, worms, beetles, carrion, eggs and nestlings. They normally live alone and can walk for several kilometres at night as they look for food. These small animals are preyed upon by badgers and foxes. Hedgehogs hibernate from October to April in compost heaps and bonfire piles. They can be injured accidentally by gardeners.

FACT FILE

Scientific name
Erinaceus europaeus

Size 20–30 cm

Weight 1–2 kg

Habitat Woodlands, farms, parks, gardens, hedges

Breeding In spring, 2–7 young

Young hedgehogs are born blind and helpless. Their mother cares for them for four weeks before they can leave the nest.

Rounded body covered with yellow-tipped spines

Pointed face

Coarse fur underneath

Short legs and feet equipped with sharp claws for digging

MOLE

It is unusual to see moles as they spend most of their lives underground, digging or sleeping. They have soft, dense, grey-black fur, pink noses, whiskers, and very small eyes. They eat earthworms and insect grubs, which they find using their excellent senses of smell and hearing. They store hundreds of worms in underground larders so they have a ready supply of food.

FACT FILE

Scientific name
Talpa europaea

Size 11–16 cm

Weight 70–130 g

Habitat Woodlands, fields, parks, gardens

Breeding From February to June

Moles are well known for their digging skills. They use their shovel-like forelimbs to scoop earth away to create a tunnel.

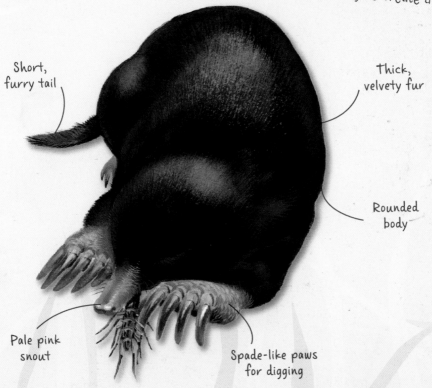

Short, furry tail

Thick, velvety fur

Rounded body

Pale pink snout

Spade-like paws for digging

COMMON SHREW

Common shrews may be one of the most abundant mammals in Britain. However, they are so secretive, you may never spot one unless you know where to look. These little furry animals are experts at remaining hidden beneath vegetation, and they have to spend most of their lives looking for food and eating. With a good sense of smell, shrews can detect prey up to 12 cm underground. They are most active at night, and are preyed upon by owls.

FACT FILE

Scientific name *Sorex araneus*
Size 5–8 cm
Weight 5–12 g
Habitat Woodlands, hedgerows, grasslands
Breeding 2–4 litters a year

Common shrews don't like company! If they bump into each other they freeze, then squeak and stand up on their hind legs before running away.

Dark brown, soft, silky fur

Pointed snout

Small eyes

Pale fur underneath

PYGMY SHREW

These small, rodent-like mammals are often found near compost heaps in gardens. Pygmy shrews run away quickly when disturbed, making it difficult to identify them for sure – at first glance, they look like young mice or rats. Pygmy shrews are common visitors to gardens and they are the UK's smallest mammal.

FACT FILE

Scientific name *Sorex minutus*

Size 4–6 cm

Weight 4–6 g

Habitat Grassland, fields, hedges, farms, gardens, parks

Breeding From April to October, 4–7 young born 23 days later

Pygmy shrews rarely live for more than one year. They may not survive harsh winters and they are preyed upon by large mammals, such as cats, foxes and stoats.

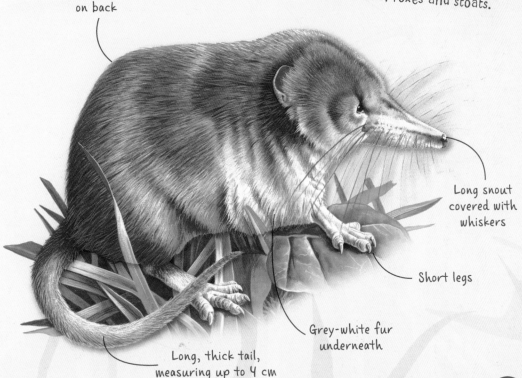

Brown fur on back

Long snout covered with whiskers

Short legs

Grey-white fur underneath

Long, thick tail, measuring up to 4 cm

WATER SHREW

This is the largest of the three British shrews and it lives near streams, rivers and ponds. It particularly likes watercress beds. Water shrews do not hibernate and are most active at night, when they dive underwater in search of small creatures to eat. Their fur is waterproof and holds bubbles of air, giving this small mammal a silvery appearance when underwater.

FACT FILE

Scientific name
Neomys fodiens

Size 6.5–9.5 cm

Weight 12–19 g

Habitat Ponds, rivers

Breeding Up to three litters of 3–14 young are born in summer

Water shrews' teeth contain iron. This hard metal makes the teeth tough and less likely to wear down, despite chewing and gnawing. It gives them a red tinge at the tips.

White tufts of fur near eyes and ears

Black fur on back

Long, sensitive snout

Long tail

Whitish fur underneath

COMMON PIPISTRELLE

Pipistrelles are the smallest and most common bats in the UK. They are unlikely to be spotted in winter, but during summer they swoop and dive, with a characteristic jerky flight, over gardens. They roost in buildings, and can squeeze through tiny gaps to find somewhere sheltered and dry to rest. They feed on flying insects, and one bat can eat more than 3000 insects in one night.

FACT FILE

Scientific name
Pipistrellus pipistrellus

Size 19–25 cm (wingspan)

Weight 3–10 g

Habitat Almost all habitats, except very open places

Breeding 1–2 young in autumn

In Britain, female pipistrelles usually give birth to just one young, but in central Europe, twins are much more common.

Narrow wings

Digits (fingers) on each wing

Large, black ears

Strong claws on the feet enable the bat to hang upside down when roosting

Body covered in brown fur

Bats • MAMMALS (53)

DAUBENTON'S BAT

These common bats live near sources of water, such as canals, reservoirs and rivers. At twilight they can sometimes be spotted swooping down to the water's surface, chasing insects at speeds of about 25 km/h. Their diet is mostly made up of midges, caddis flies and mayflies. In summer they roost in tree holes, bridges and caves. Up to 200 bats may live in one colony.

FACT FILE

Scientific name
Myotis daubentonii

Size 24–27 cm (wingspan)

Weight 7–15 g

Habitat Near water

Breeding Mating in autumn, females give birth in summer

Like other bats, Daubenton's bat makes sounds that it uses to locate its prey and judge its distance and size. This is called echolocation.

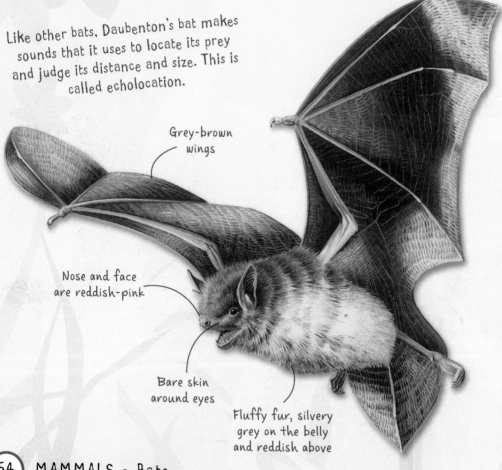

Grey-brown wings

Nose and face are reddish-pink

Bare skin around eyes

Fluffy fur, silvery grey on the belly and reddish above

NOCTULE

Noctule bats emerge from their resting places in the early evening, before the sun has completely set. They hunt for insects, such as moths and beetles. They are fast fliers and can dart around, diving or changing direction swiftly. It is harder to find noctules in winter, as they either migrate south to warmer places or hibernate. They can live to 12 years of age and are found in England and Wales only.

FACT FILE

Scientific name
Nyctalus noctula
Size 32–45 cm (wingspan)
Weight 20–40 g
Habitat Woodlands, parks
Breeding One young born in June or early July

Noctules huddle together during their winter hibernations to keep warm. However, in very cold weather, half of all the bats in a colony may freeze to death.

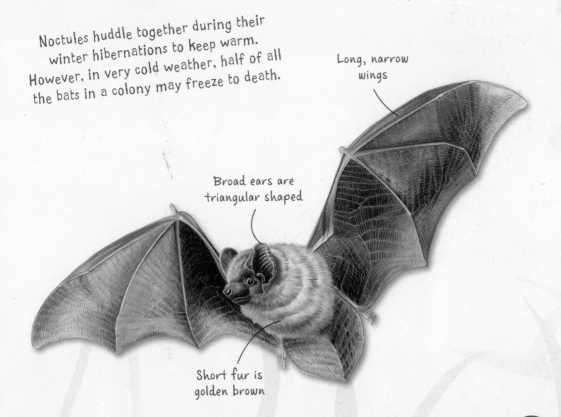

Long, narrow wings

Broad ears are triangular shaped

Short fur is golden brown

BROWN LONG-EARED BAT

Like most other bats, brown long-eared bats live on a diet of insects. They come out at night and dart around the skies on the hunt for food. Their hearing is so good that these small mammals can detect a single insect on the ground just by the noise it makes as it walks. Brown long-eared bats are also known as whispering bats because the calls they make are very quiet.

FACT FILE

Scientific name
Plecotus aurius

Size 24–28 cm (wingspan)

Weight 5–15 g

Habitat Woodlands, orchards, parks

Breeding One young in June

Long-eared bats deserve their name because their ears measure three-quarters the length of their bodies. That's like a human having ears that reach to their knees!

Wing membrane is pale grey-brown

Long ears, joined at the base

Small eyes (but bats have good eyesight)

Fur is greyish-brown above and yellowish below

HARVEST MOUSE

The European harvest mouse is the smallest rodent in Britain. It has an extraordinary tail, which it uses like a fifth limb. A harvest mouse can wrap its tail around grass stems, using it for balance, climbing and grasping. They eat grass, berries, cereals, fruit, insects and seeds. Harvest mice are at risk from pesticides and combine harvesters, but their natural predators include crows, cats and weasels.

FACT FILE

Scientific name
Micromys minutus

Size 5–6 cm

Weight 4–6 g

Habitat Dry grasslands, fields

Breeding 3–7 litters a year, with 1–8 young in each

The spherical nests built by pregnant females are very complicated structures. They are woven from grass and can measure 10 cm in diameter.

Small, rounded ears

Golden-brown fur

Blunt nose

Mainly white underside

Broad feet with gripping toes

Long, grasping tail

HOUSE MOUSE

Although mice are very common mammals, it is unusual to see them because they are most active at night. House mice first came from Asia, but they are now found around the world, almost anywhere that humans live. During winter they may come into houses, often setting up home in roof spaces, under floorboards or in outbuildings.

Mice are small rodents and are able to fit into the smallest of spaces to search for food, such as seeds, berries, snails and spiders.

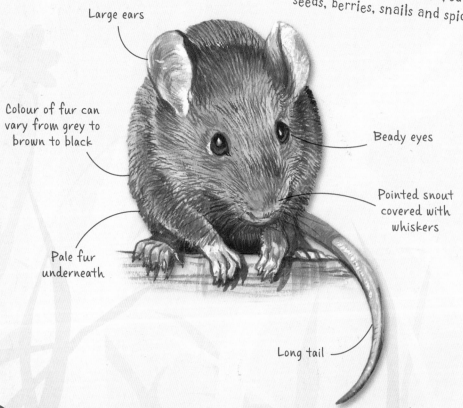

Large ears

Colour of fur can vary from grey to brown to black

Beady eyes

Pointed snout covered with whiskers

Pale fur underneath

Long tail

WOOD MOUSE

Although wood mice are normally nocturnal, they may be spotted during daylight hours at breeding times. They eat a wide range of food, including moss, seeds, small insects and nuts. Males are very aggressive and often fight one another to protect their territories. They have even been known to kill young mice. The wood mouse is also known as the long-tailed field mouse.

FACT FILE

Scientific name
Apodemus sylvaticus

Size 8–10 cm

Weight 13–27 g

Habitat Widespread in most habitats

Breeding Seven litters every year, with 2–9 young in each

Large ears and eyes

Brown or chestnut fur

Wood mice have orangey-brown fur. They sometimes enter houses looking for food. They are good climbers and can often be spotted in trees.

White or grey belly

YELLOW-NECKED MOUSE

It is easy to confuse wood mice and yellow-necked mice as they are very similar in size and appearance. The only distinguishing mark is the patch of yellow fur on a yellow-necked mouse's neck, but this is often difficult to spot – especially as mice are fast-movers! Yellow-necked mice are mostly nocturnal and are excellent climbers. They eat seeds, fruit, buds and seedlings. These mice live in some regions of England and Wales.

FACT FILE

Scientific name
Apodermus flavicollis

Size 9–12.5 cm

Weight 15–45 g

Habitat Woodlands, gardens, orchards

Breeding Three litters in summer, 2–11 young in each

When the young are born they are blind and helpless. They open their eyes when they are about 16 days old, and just five days later they are completely independent.

Brown fur

Bib of yellowish fur on the chest

Long tail

White or cream belly

BROWN RAT

These rodents live almost everywhere that humans live. They are found in towns, cities and the countryside – anywhere they can find food. They are often associated with dirty places, such as rubbish heaps and sewers, but rats also live in hedgerows and fields. They are highly intelligent creatures with natural curiosity. They can live in large groups, or colonies, and fight one another for the best territory.

FACT FILE

Scientific name
Rattus norvegicus
Size 11–28 cm
Weight 200–400 g
Habitat All habitats, especially farmland
Breeding Five litters a year

Compost heaps are a perfect place for rats to breed. The compost keeps them warm and there is a steady supply of food.

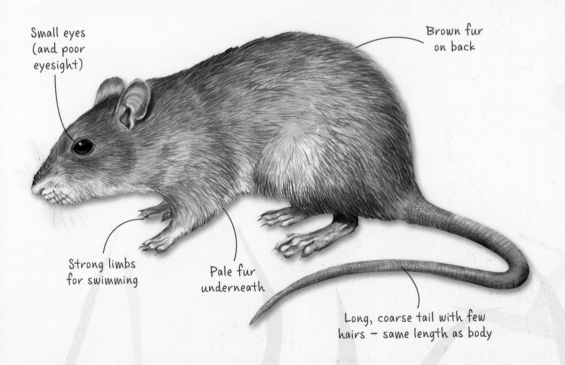

Small eyes (and poor eyesight)

Brown fur on back

Strong limbs for swimming

Pale fur underneath

Long, coarse tail with few hairs – same length as body

BANK VOLE

At first glance, a vole can easily be mistaken for a mouse. However, if they stay still long enough, their plump bodies, smaller ears and short, furry tails are obvious. Bank voles live in woodland, hedgerows, parks and gardens where they eat fruit, nuts and small insects. They are very active animals, and are frequently seen, sometimes even visiting bird tables. They are eaten by weasels, stoats, foxes and birds of prey.

FACT FILE

Scientific name
Clethrionomys glareolus
Size 9–12 cm
Weight 20–45 g
Habitat Grasslands
Breeding Can give birth to their first litter of 3–8 young when only five weeks old

Bank voles live dangerous lives and few survive more than five months. They are not only hunted by other animals, but males often die after fighting one another.

Short fur, rusty brown on the back with greyish sides

Small eyes

Rounded snout

Short tail

White fur underneath

FIELD VOLE

Also known as short-tailed voles, field voles are one of Britain's most common mammals, although they are rarely spotted. They are very common in grassland, as well as heathland and moorland where they feed on seeds, roots and leaves. They spend much more of their time in runs and burrows and are less likely to be seen than bank voles. Field voles are eaten by many predators, especially kestrels and barn owls. The field vole is a sandier brown colour than the bank vole with a shorter tail.

FACT FILE

Scientific name
Microtus agrestis
Size 8–13 cm
Weight 15–50 g
Habitat Rough grassland, woodland, fields, hedges
Breeding Mating from March to October

One female can have up to five litters a year. If each litter contains five babies, this is a total of 25 babies a year!

Short fur, grey-brown or sandy on the back

Small ears

Short, furry tail

Blunt snout

Pale fur on underside

WATER VOLE

These voles were once commonplace in Britain, but their numbers have dropped dramatically in recent years. It is thought that this is because their riverside habitats have been destroyed or polluted, and because American minks hunt them – causing their extinction in some areas. These mammals eat plants growing by the water's edge and are excellent swimmers. Water voles are also known as water rats.

Young female water voles can force their mothers to leave the burrows by hitting them with their tails or even boxing them with their forefeet!

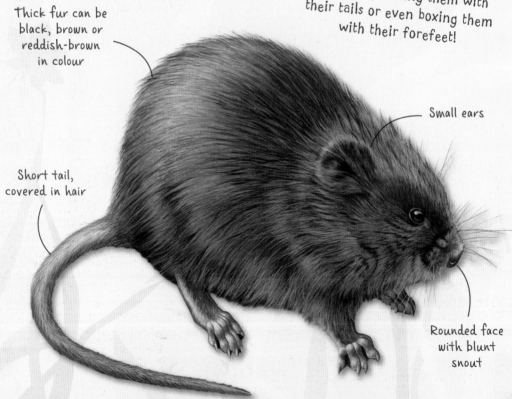

Thick fur can be black, brown or reddish-brown in colour

Small ears

Short tail, covered in hair

Rounded face with blunt snout

DORMOUSE

Dormice spend up to three-quarters of their lives sleeping, and much of that time is spent in hibernation. A long sleep over winter is a good way to save energy when there is little food around. However, when they are active, dormice are very sprightly and jump, climb and scuttle around. This rodent is also known as the hazel dormouse or common dormouse.

FACT FILE

Scientific name
Muscardinus avellanarius

Size 6–9 cm

Weight 15–30 g

Habitat Woodlands, shrubbery

Breeding From May to October, 2–7 young per litter

This animal is known for its sleepiness — and that's how it got its name. The 'dor' part comes from the French verb 'dormir', which means 'to sleep'.

Golden fur on back

Large eyes

Paler fur on underside

Long, fluffy tail

RED SQUIRREL

These squirrels are smaller than their grey cousins. They are much harder to spot nowadays because there are only a few places in Britain where they have been able to survive. They usually live in woodlands with conifer trees, where they can chew on pine cones and nibble pine seeds. They also eat leaves, fruit, buds and insects. Red squirrels build nests, called dreys, which are made from a frame of twigs, lined with soft plants.

FACT FILE

Scientific name
Sciurus vulagris
Size 20–24 cm
Weight 280–350 g
Habitat Conifer woodlands
Breeding Mating in January to March, litter of three young is born 40 days later

The number of red squirrels in Britain has dropped dramatically. This is largely because they have to compete with grey squirrels for food.

Tufted ears in winter

Bushy tail

Buff or cream-coloured underneath

Colour varies from russet brown to dark brown, or grey in winter

GREY SQUIRREL

Originally from America, grey squirrels are now a common species of mammal, found in parks, gardens and woodland habitats. They have stocky bodies covered in thick, grey fur, and long arching tails. They are active during the day, scurrying about on the ground or in trees, looking for food, such as nuts, shoots and bulbs.

Squirrels build large nests, called dreys, in trees. The outer frame is made from twigs, and the inside is then lined with dry leaves and grass.

Grey fur flecked with rust-coloured hair

No tufts of fur on tips of ears (unlike red squirrels)

Short front limbs with paws

White fur underneath

Long, bushy tail

BROWN HARE

Very fast runners, brown hares can reach speeds of 60 km/h when trying to escape a predator. Brown hares have orangey-brown fur and long slender ears with black tips. Hares are herbivores (they only eat plants). They are hunted by foxes and young hares may be caught by birds of prey. Hares are often found in open grassland and may wander into nearby gardens, but they are easily scared away.

FACT FILE

Scientific name
Lepus europaeus

Size 50–80 cm

Weight 4–7 kg

Habitat Grasslands, farms, hedgerows

Breeding Up to three litters every year, with 1–4 young

Courtship takes place in spring, giving rise to the phrase 'mad March hare'. Females stand on their hind legs and 'box' males to keep them away.

Ears are similar length to head

Black-tipped ears

Orangey-brown fur

White chest fur

Long limbs for quick movement

MOUNTAIN HARE

Unlike its cousins, the brown hare and the rabbit, the mountain hare is native to Britain but is found only in Scotland and northern regions of England. These hares are most likely to be spotted alone, in the early morning or at dusk. Occasionally a group may feed together. They eat grasses, heather, rushes and herbs, and are preyed upon by foxes, stoats, cats and birds of prey. The mountain hare is also known as the blue hare or white hare.

FACT FILE

Scientific name *Lepus timidus*
Size 45–66 cm
Weight 2–6 kg
Habitat Forests, moorlands
Breeding 1–4 litters a year, with 1–5 young in each

A female mountain hare can produce up to 25 young, called leverets, in a breeding season. If she lives for nine years, she could have several hundred offspring!

Ears tipped with black

Coat is brown in summer, white in winter

Slender, agile body

Tail stays white throughout the year

Long legs and large feet

Rabbits & Hares • MAMMALS (69)

RABBIT

The European rabbit was brought to Britain by the Normans in the 11th century to provide fur and meat. Since then, they have settled so well that many people regard them as pests. Rabbits eat plant matter, such as grass, crops, cereals and young trees. They live in burrows that connect together to make a warren. Young rabbits are called kittens.

Myxomatosis is a rabbit disease that reached Britain in the 1950s. It killed nearly all the wild British rabbits. The disease still exists, but not to such a deadly degree.

Long ears with black tips (but shorter than hares' ears)

Eyes on either side of head

Coat can be grey, brown, sandy yellow or black

White underneath

RED FOX

Once mainly found in the countryside, red foxes are now widespread in towns and cities – where they have discovered a new source of food. They often scavenge from rubbish bins and will eat almost any food they find lying around. Females are called vixens and are smaller than males, which are called dogs. Foxes are most active at night, especially at dawn and dusk.

FACT FILE

Scientific name *Vulpes vulpes*
Size 50–80 cm
Weight 2–7 kg
Habitat Fields, scrubland, gardens, parks, along railways
Breeding Mate mid-winter and 4–5 cubs are born 52 days later

Cubs are born completely blind in early spring. When they are a few months old, they can often be seen playing in gardens.

Reddish-brown fur (may be mangy, dirty or patchy)

Black fur on ears

Long, thick tail, known as a 'brush'

White chest and throat

BADGER

These animals live in the countryside, in woodland and on large commons. Badgers occasionally wander into gardens and farmland, but as they are nocturnal, seeing a badger is rare. If they come close to human homes, they may be searching for food and will scavenge in rubbish bins. Badgers are omnivorous – they eat both meat and plants. Male badgers are called boars, the females are called sows, and their young are known as cubs.

FACT FILE

Scientific name *Meles meles*

Size 67–90 cm

Weight 8–12 kg

Habitat Woodland, farmland, parks, other open areas

Breeding Most cubs are born January to March

Badgers use their strong claws and powerful legs to dig up bee and wasp nests in order to feed on honey and larvae.

Short tail (females have bushier tails than males)

Thick, coarse, slate-grey fur

Small, pointed head and short neck

Short, strong legs with sharp claws for digging

Black stripes mark its white face

OTTER

Sighting an otter by a riverbank is a rare treat. These animals are very shy and likely to disappear beneath the water's surface when they are disturbed. They mostly feed on fish, but they will also eat water birds and frogs. Otters find it hard to survive in polluted water and this has affected their numbers in recent years. They have also been hunted for their fur and to stop them eating fish.

Otter cubs need a helping hand to learn how to fish. Their mother catches a fish and then releases it in front of the cubs, so they can practise capturing it for themselves.

Smooth, brown fur

Long, slender body

Pale on underside

Short legs

Webbed feet

Thick tail

PINE MARTEN

Pine martens are nocturnal mammals, which means they are most active at night and usually sleep during the day. They make their dens in tree holes, old squirrel nests and rocky crevices. They eat a wide range of food, depending on what is available – from rodents and birds to eggs, beetles and berries. They are excellent climbers but hunt on the ground. Pine martens live in very few areas of Britain outside of Scotland.

FACT FILE

Scientific name *Martes martes*
Size 45–55 cm
Weight 1–2.2 kg
Habitat Woodlands, cliffs
Breeding 1–5 cubs born in spring

Pine martens were brought close to extinction during the 18th and 19th centuries. They were killed for their fur and to stop them preying upon chickens and game birds.

Big ears

Large eyes

Pointed muzzle

Creamy yellow patch of fur on chest

Dark to light-brown fur

Long, fluffy tail

Polecats are easy to identify because they have characteristic markings on their faces. However, they are hard to spot because they only come out during the day when they are struggling to find food, and are normally active at dusk or night. Polecats are carnivores, which means they eat meat. They hunt rabbits, rodents, frogs, toads and birds, but will eat insects, too. These mammals are found in England and Wales.

FACT FILE

Scientific name
Mustela putorius
Size 35–51 cm
Weight 0.7–1.5 kg
Habitat Marshes, woods, riverbanks
Breeding A single litter of 3–7 young born May to June

In the times of Queen Elizabeth I, about 450 years ago, polecats were regarded as bloodthirsty vermin, or pests. They were hunted mercilessly and nearly became extinct.

Broad head

Slender body

Dark coat

Black, mask-like markings

Short legs

STOAT

These mammals are closely related to weasels, pine martens, otters, minks and badgers. However, stoats are larger than weasels and have reddish-brown fur. In northern parts of the UK, their fur turns white in winter. They can climb trees, swim and jump. Stoats use their excellent sense of smell to find their prey, which they kill with a single bite to the back of the neck. Thanks to their long and slender bodies, stoats can chase their prey into burrows.

In winter, stoats were once hunted for their ermine pelts (fur), which were used to make stoles and robes worn by royalty and judges. Nowadays, artificial fur is used.

FACT FILE

Scientific name
Mustela erminea
Size 23–30 cm
Weight 1–4 kg
Habitat Farms, woodland, parks, grasslands, scrubland
Breeding Mates in summer and a litter of 6–12 in spring

Small eyes and ears

White fur underneath

Reddish-brown fur on back

Long, slender body

Black-tipped tail

WEASEL

Found in woods, farms and large gardens, weasels are active both at night and during the day. They sleep in burrows that have been abandoned by badgers or rabbits. Weasels live alone and mark their territory with strong scent. They are busy mammals and need to eat regularly to maintain their energy levels – they cannot survive more than 24 hours without food.

FACT FILE

Scientific name
Mustela nivalis
Size 15–25 cm
Weight 50–100 g
Habitat Woodland, farms, gardens
Breeding Mates from spring to autumn, 3–8 young

Weasels sometimes leap around strangely. It was thought they did this to confuse their prey, but it actually may be due to a worm that lives in weasels' noses.

Small, flattened head

Long, slender body

Brown fur on back

White fur underneath

Short legs

COMMON SEAL

Nearly half of the European population of common seals live around the coast of Britain, usually in sheltered waters. These large mammals often come to land, hauling themselves awkwardly onto rocky shores, mudflats and sand bars. Here, their pups are protected from predators, such as foxes and birds of prey. The common seal is also known as the harbour seal.

FACT FILE

Scientific name *Phoca vitulina*
Size Up to 2 m
Weight 45–175 kg
Habitat Coastal waters of the North Atlantic Ocean
Breeding Adults mate underwater and single pups are born

Seals need to breathe in air, but they can hold their breath for up to ten minutes when they dive below water, searching for fish to eat.

Colour varies and can be black, brown, tan or grey

Large head

Short body

Short flippers

Nostrils form a 'V' shape

BOTTLENOSE DOLPHIN

The sight of a group of bottlenose dolphins leaping out of the water is an unforgettable treat. These mammals are social animals and often appear near the coast in a group, or school. Sometimes it is possible to spy them surfing the waves, jumping several metres out of the water, or even tossing seaweed around in what appears to be a game. Bottlenose dolphins are also known as grey porpoises, black porpoises and cowfish.

FACT FILE

Scientific name
Tursiops truncatis

Size 1.9–4 m

Weight Up to 650 kg

Habitat Ocean, harbours, bays, river mouths

Breeding Calving takes place all year round

Bottlenose dolphins live in oceans and seas around the world. Those found around the coast of Britain are among the largest and heaviest of all.

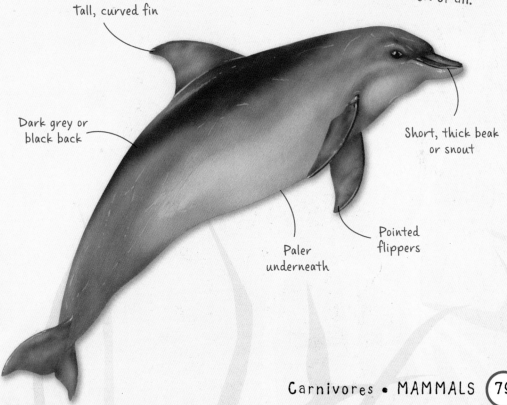

Tall, curved fin

Dark grey or black back

Short, thick beak or snout

Paler underneath

Pointed flippers

ROE DEER

This is an elegant, small deer that originally comes from Scotland, but has been introduced to other parts of Britain. It is easiest to see roe deer at dawn and dusk when they are less likely to be resting or hiding. They lose their antlers between October and January. When the new antlers grow, they are covered in soft 'velvet', which provides blood to help them develop.

FACT FILE

Scientific name
Capreolus capreolus

Size Up to 75 cm (to shoulder)

Weight Up to 25 kg

Habitat Grassland, woodland, moors

Breeding 1–3 fawns (called kids) are born in May or June

Young fawns are left alone all day while their parents feed. Their spotted coats help them hide from predators. At six weeks, they follow their mothers everywhere.

Male's antlers usually have three points

Black muzzle band

White chin and throat patches

Large, white rump

Reddish fur in summer, grey-brown-black in winter

RED DEER

Red deer are the largest land-living mammals that are native to Britain, but they are mostly restricted to parts of Scotland. The females are called hinds, the males are called stags and the young are called fawns. Red deer stags have the largest antlers of any British deer, and they can reach an impressive one metre in width. Stags and hinds often spend their time in separate groups, coming together only at breeding time.

In autumn, stags fight to mate with the most females. During this time, which is called 'the rut', they roar, lock antlers, push and twist. Fights can cause injury or death.

Rump has a patch of cream-coloured fur

Multi-branched antlers

Reddish-brown coat in summer, dull brown in winter

FALLOW DEER

Most fallow deer live in parks where they are protected, but some live wild. They are particularly active at dawn and dusk, but they spend much of their time grazing. During the mating season, males can become very aggressive and they fight one another to get more does, or females, in their group. Fallow deer are sometimes farmed for their meat, which is called venison.

The Normans brought fallow deer to England in the 11th century. Large deer parks were set up in medieval times so members of the royal family could hunt them.

Large, broad, flat antlers

Tan-coloured coat with white spotting

White rump

Yellowish-white underneath

DARTMOOR PONY

Dartmoor ponies have survived on the moors of southwest England for at least 1000 years. These animals are not pure-bred, but have been crossed with Thoroughbreds and Arabs to improve the breed. Dartmoors are also bred for use as childrens' riding ponies. They have gentle natures, making them suitable for children learning to ride and care for a pony.

FACT FILE

Scientific name *Equus caballus*

Size 100–120 cm (to shoulder)

Weight 200–250 kg

Habitat Moors

Breeding Foals born between May and August

Dartmoor ponies were bred at a prison in the 1900s, up until 1960. The guards used them to transport prisoners to and from jail.

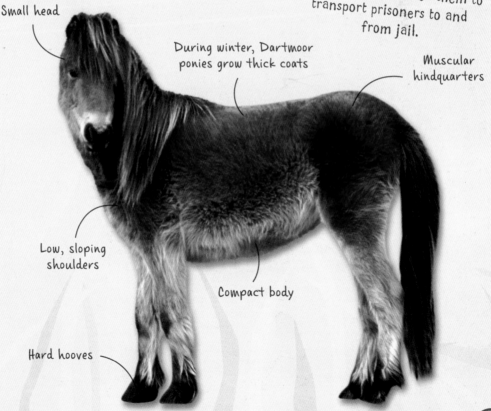

Small head

During winter, Dartmoor ponies grow thick coats

Muscular hindquarters

Low, sloping shoulders

Compact body

Hard hooves

FULMAR

The fulmar is a true sea bird that never feeds on land. It can glide like an albatross on stiff wings over one metre wide, staying close to the sea surface. It is found all around the British coast, wherever there are cliffs for it to nest. The fulmar spends most of its time at sea, and is an enthusiastic follower of fishing boats. A large increase in British fulmar numbers in the 20th century may have been due to plentiful supplies of fish waste and offal from trawlers and whalers.

FACT FILE

Scientific name
Fulmarus glacialis

Size 45–50 cm

Wingspan 100–110 cm

Call Cackling 'ag-ag-ag-arrr'

Breeding Single white egg

Grey upperparts

Yellow bill

White breast

Square, short tail

Fulmars defend their nests energetically, and may eject a foul-smelling 'fulmar oil' at persistent intruders.

MANX SHEARWATER

The Manx shearwater elegantly skims the waves, following the water contours, tipping first one way, then the other. It breeds mainly on islands off the Irish coast and the English west coast. It has a habit of congregating on the water below the breeding site at dusk, not coming ashore until after dark, possibly to avoid predators. Its food includes fish, crustaceans and invertebrates that it picks off the sea surface. It has no trouble navigating back to its nest-site, which is in a deep burrow.

FACT FILE

Scientific name
Puffinus puffinus

Size 30–38 cm

Wingspan 70–85 cm

Call 'Kookoo- kooroo'

Breeding Single egg, in May

Thin, short
black bill

Dark back

White
underparts

With its effortless, gliding flight, the Manx shearwater can travel great distances to feed, sometimes as much as 300 km.

STORM PETREL

The storm petrel, no larger than a sparrow, stays at sea most of its life. It survives the stormiest weather despite its small size. Storm petrels have learned to follow ships, fluttering over the wake to pick up scraps. Their natural food is plankton, tiny animal and plant organisms, which they harvest from the sea surface. In its breeding season the storm petrel goes ashore after dark to its breeding sites on islands on the western coasts of Scotland and Ireland, and on the Northern Isles.

Sailors once called storm petrels Mother Carey's chickens, and thought that large numbers of them foretold approaching bad weather.

All black

White rump

Square tail

GANNET

The gannet is one of the most spectacular diving birds in northern Atlantic waters. Plummeting down from heights of up to 40 m at speeds approaching 100 km/h, the gannet folds its wings as it approaches the water, piercing the sea surface like an arrow. It is helped in this by a lack of external nostrils, which could take up water from the impact. With a wingspan of almost 2 m, it is one of our largest sea birds. It locates its prey from a great height, especially shoals of herring and mackerel.

Fishermen have often been guided to good fishing areas by the sight of diving gannets.

Yellow crown

Pointed white tail

Black wing-tips

CORMORANT

Cormorants are unusual looking water birds, with angular bodies and dark feathers. They are superb swimmers and live all over Britain in watery habitats, especially by the coast. When a cormorant catches a fish it brings it to the water's surface and shakes it vigorously, before swallowing it. Cormorants have large webbed feet that they use for swimming and for hatching their eggs, which they hold between the top of their feet and their warm bodies.

FACT FILE

Scientific name
Phalacrocorax carbo

Size 90 cm

Wingspan 130–160 cm

Call Growling and cackling

Breeding 3–4 eggs, in April

When cormorants perch to dry themselves they have an unusual body position, or stance. They stand up straight with their wings half open and their neck upright.

Glossy back

Long, hooked yellow bill

White cheeks and chin

Long, broad tail

White patch in summer

SHAG

The shag is smaller and slimmer than its relative, the cormorant, with proportionally shorter wings and neck. It stays on wild, rocky coasts, and does not venture inland. It is more at home in rough, deep waters than the cormorant, flying very close to the sea surface whatever the weather. It is a skilful and agile underwater swimmer, and feeds on shoal fish such as herrings and sand eels. The shag times its breeding so that the hatchlings appear at around the same time that sand eels are most plentiful.

FACT FILE

Scientific name
Phalacrocorax aristotelis
Size 76 cm
Wingspan 95–110 cm
Call 'Karr' and 'arrk-arrk'
Breeding Three eggs, late spring

The shag often springs entirely clear of the water before diving for fish.

Crest

Black bill with yellow gape

Metallic, greenish-black plumage

GREY HERON

The stately grey heron is found all over the British Isles, and is a familiar sight standing patiently in marshes and the shallows of lakes and rivers. Its prey is usually fish, but it also catches frogs, worms, insects and small mammals. Usually the only time it appears in the garden is when it drops in to clear out the resident goldfish from the garden pond. The grey heron nests in colonies in the canopies of tall trees.

FACT FILE

Scientific name
Ardea cinerea
Size 90–98 cm
Wingspan 175–200 cm
Call 'Kraak', and 'krreik'
in flight
Breeding 2–7 eggs, from
February

It either stalks its prey with very slow movements, or waits motionless in order to surprise it with a sudden strike of its powerful, pointed beak.

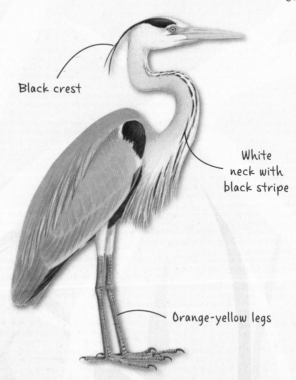

Black crest

White neck with black stripe

Orange-yellow legs

MUTE SWAN

There are three types of swan that can be seen in Britain – mute, Bewick's and whooper. Mute swans are the only ones that are resident all year round. These large waterbirds mate for life. The male is called a cob, the female is a pen and the young are called cygnets. Both parents incubate the eggs and, once hatched, the cygnets sometimes ride around on their parents' backs. Mute swans eat vegetation from the riverbed, which they reach with their long necks.

FACT FILE

Scientific name *Cygnus olor*
Size 140–160 cm
Wingspan 200–235 cm
Call Loud trumpet or hiss
Breeding Up to eight eggs, from March to June

Swans were once regarded as valuable birds and were traded between noblemen. Today, the Queen owns British mute swans and still employs a Swan Keeper.

Large black swelling at base of bill

Long, elegant, curved neck

Adult plumage is all white (but brown in cygnets)

Orange-red bill

CANADA GOOSE

These geese originally came to Britain from North America. They quickly settled in and are now established all over the country, except in the most northern areas. They are often considered a nuisance because they gather together in large, noisy groups. Males and females form lifelong pairs – this behaviour is described as monogamy, which means having just one mating partner. A pair stays together to look after the eggs and the young, which are called goslings.

FACT FILE

Scientific name
Branta candadensis
Size 90–110 cm
Wingspan 130–180 cm
Call Deep loud 'ah-ronk'
Breeding 5–6 eggs, in spring, hatching around 25 days later

The edges of a Canada goose's bill are lined with special 'teeth' called lamellae. These are used to cut grass or other vegetation.

Black bill

Body is swan-shaped

White chinstrap

White patch under tail

Black legs

Pale breast

BRENT GOOSE

The brent goose eats plant food for the most part, feeding on eel grass, algae and marsh plants in the salt marshes and muddy estuaries where it grazes. It also eats young cereal plants, and picks up the fallen grain from stubble after harvesting. There are two branches of the brent goose family. The dark-bellied birds fly to southern British estuaries from Russia. The pale-bellied birds fly from Greenland to Ireland, and from Spitzbergen to northeast England. The brent goose is the smallest of the European geese.

FACT FILE

Scientific name
Branta bernicla

Size 55–60 cm

Wingspan 110–120 cm

Call 'Rronk-rronk'

Breeding 3–5 eggs in a clutch

Like most geese, this bird enjoys company, and feeds, flies and roosts in close-packed flocks.

White neck-flash

Dark belly

White rump

SHELDUCK

The colourful shelduck pairs up with its mate for more than one season. The pair establishes separate nesting and feeding territories, often a considerable distance apart. The female shelduck chooses a burrow in which to lay her eggs. When the young are hatched the parents escort them on what can be a long walk to the water where they can feed. They travel in single file, with one parent leading, and the other bringing up the rear.

FACT FILE

Scientific name
Tadorna tadorna
Size 60–70 cm
Wingspan 110–115 cm
Call Male, low whistle, 'huee'.
Female, deep rapid quacks,
'ak-ak-ak'
Breeding 8–10 eggs in a clutch

The shelduck is the largest duck in the British Isles, feeding mainly on muddy estuaries and sandy shores. Its broad bill acts as a sieve for separating molluscs from mud.

Dark green head

Red bill with knob

Rusty coloured band on chest

LONG-TAILED DUCK

The long-tailed duck is a winter visitor. It is seen most commonly between northeast England and the Shetland Islands, and in the Outer Hebrides. A large proportion – up to 75 percent – of the British winter population lives around the waters and inlets of the Moray Firth. The long-tailed duck breeds in northern tundra lands, moving south to winter on the sea. It dives for its food of molluscs and crustaceans, and prefers to spend its winter break in shallow waters.

FACT FILE

Scientific name
Clangula hyemalis
Size 40–53 cm
Wingspan 70–80 cm
Call 'Calloo'
Breeding 6–9 eggs in a clutch

This duck is a fast flier, and has no fear of harsh weather conditions, swimming and diving however rough the sea.

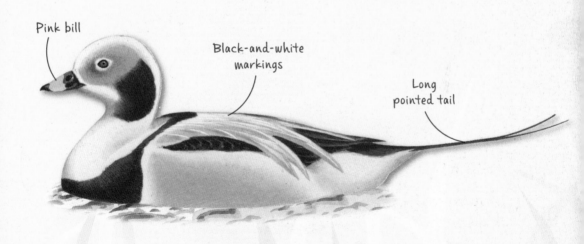

Pink bill

Black-and-white markings

Long pointed tail

TEAL

Many of the teals in Britain stay here all year round. However, a number of them travel here from Siberia and northwest Europe for winter, especially in central and western areas. These are the smallest British surface-feeding ducks, and they often live together in groups ranging in size from 20 to several hundred. These small ducks are quick and agile, and move easily around the edges of the water, searching for vegetation to eat.

Male teals, called drakes, may put on displays of head-bobbing to impress a female. These displays help females choose the best and healthiest mates.

Chestnut head with green band over eye

White or cream stripe on wing

Bright green patches of feathers on the hindwings

Grey speckled plumage on body

Yellow triangle below tail

MALLARD

The mallard is the largest and most familiar of the dabbling ducks. It can be seen on village ponds and park lakes as well as marshes and rivers all through the year. The male is a handsome bird, with a glossy green head, chestnut breast and grey body. Females are much less colourful, and well camouflaged, being mottled grey and brown. They feed on vegetation, seeds, small invertebrates and will famously feed on bread.

FACT FILE

Scientific name
Anas platyrhynchos

Size 50–60 cm

Wingspan 80–95 cm

Call Loud 'quack'

Breeding Up to 12 eggs, March to July

The mallard is the commonest species of duck in the world, numbering up to 19 million birds, and the ancestor of almost all breeds of domestic and farmyard ducks.

Emerald-green head

Yellow bill

Chesnut-brown chest

Cream body

COMMON SCOTER

The male common scoter is the only duck with totally black plumage. Common scoters breed on lakes and pools in the Arctic tundra, and move to sea coasts in winter. They feed by diving for molluscs, especially mussels. A few pairs breed on lakes in Scotland, but most common scoters that appear in British waters are winter visitors seen swimming and feeding off the coast. They are often in the company of velvet scoters.

The common scoter spends most of its time at sea. It is capable of diving to great depths and stays under water for up to one minute at a time.

Yellow bill with black knob at base

All-black plumage

VELVET SCOTER

The velvet scoter visits the British Isles in winter. It is bigger and heavier than its relative, the common scoter. It is often seen close to the shore. Velvet scoters tend to be seen in small flocks, sometimes mixed in with common scoters. On land the velvet scoter is awkward, and rarely comes ashore in Britain. It is an accomplished swimmer and diver, reaching depths of up to 20 m. It feeds on molluscs and crustaceans when at sea, but during its Arctic breeding season includes roots and water plants in its diet.

FACT FILE

Scientific name
Melanitta fusca
Size 51–58 cm
Wingspan 90–95 cm
Call Male, piping call, 'kyu'. Female, hoarse, churring 'braaa'
Breeding 8–9 eggs in a clutch

The velvet scoter has been timed under water at up to three minutes.

Large yellow bill

White eye-patch

White wing-patch

RED-BREASTED MERGANSER

The red-breasted merganser is a bird of inlets, shallow coastal waters, inland lakes and rivers. It is a resident breeder in Ireland and Scotland, with some pairs in northwest England and Wales. It is a saw-billed duck, so named because it has a serrated edge to its beak, which helps it to keep a grip on fish caught under water. It flies low and fast over the water surface, and is often seen swimming along with its head submerged as it scans for fish.

FACT FILE

Scientific name
Mergus serrator

Size 52–58 cm

Wingspan 70–80 cm

Call Male 'yiuv' and 'orr'.
Female 'rok-rok-rok'

Breeding 8–10 eggs in a clutch

After diving and catching a fish, the red–breasted merganser brings it to the surface to swallow it. Then it performs a wing–flapping display, followed by a drink of sea water.

Double crest

Red bill

Speckled breast

EIDER

Famous for the heat-retaining qualities of its down, the eider duck is most commonly seen in the British Isles in Scottish coastal waters. It is a resident breeder, with increasing numbers of breeding pairs in both Scotland and Ireland. Eiders dive for molluscs, often at low tide, when inshore waters are shallower. From time to time they come out of the water to rest on rocks and islets. After hatching, the ducklings are often looked after by one or more aunties, who oversee several broods.

FACT FILE

Scientific name
Somateria mollissima

Size 50–71 cm

Wingspan 90–95 cm

Call Male 'uhuu-uhuu'.
Female 'korr-korr'

Breeding 4–6 eggs

The female eider sometimes goes without food for two or three weeks while sitting on the eggs.

White back

Pink tinge to breast

Short brown legs

TUFTED DUCK

The tufted duck is one of the diving ducks, a group that feed by diving down to the bottom of deep water to catch invertebrates. They can be seen all year round, but are most common in winter, when they gather in large flocks on lakes, gravel pits and reservoirs, often together with coots and pochards. The male is black and white, while the female is a chocolate-brown all over.

FACT FILE

Scientific name *Aythya fuligula*

Size 40–45 cm

Wingspan 65–70 cm

Call Quiet growling and 'bubbling' calls

Breeding 8–11 eggs in a clutch

Tufted ducks gather in large flocks on lakes and reservoirs in winter, where their favourite food is freshwater mussels, particularly the introduced exotic Zebra Mussel.

Purple head

Long black crest

Chocolate-brown body

White chest

SCAUP

The scaup is a champion diver and swimmer that feeds in the roughest seas. It can dive for half a minute at a time to depths of around 4 m for shellfish and worms. On occasion it can stay underwater for a minute, and reach depths of 7 m. Many of the scaups overwintering around British shores are visitors from Iceland and Scandinavia, where they breed in colonies on islets in lakes and tundra pools. The scaup likes to congregate with other diving ducks.

FACT FILE

Scientific name *Aythya marila*

Size 42–51 cm

Wingspan 70–80 cm

Call Male, soft cooing courting voice. Female 'karr-karr'

Breeding 8–11 eggs in a clutch

The population of scaups has decreased dramatically in certain areas since the reduction of the waste grain that was once dumped by Scottish brewers and distillers, and which attracted huge scaup flocks.

Glossy, dark green head

Grey back

White belly

SPARROWHAWK

Sparrowhawks are becoming more common in large gardens, which is unfortunate for most visitors to the bird table, as the sparrowhawk specializes in catching small birds on the wing. When hunting, this smallish predator flies low over bushes and hedges, flapping and gliding, and weaves between tree trunks, catching its prey by surprise. The female, as in many birds of prey, is considerably larger than the male, and twice his weight.

FACT FILE

Scientific name
Accipiter nisus

Size 28–38 cm

Wingspan 60–65 cm

Call 'Kek-kek-kek'

Breeding 4–5 eggs in a clutch

Once severely reduced in numbers due to the use of agricultural pesticides, the sparrowhawk now appears to be making a come-back.

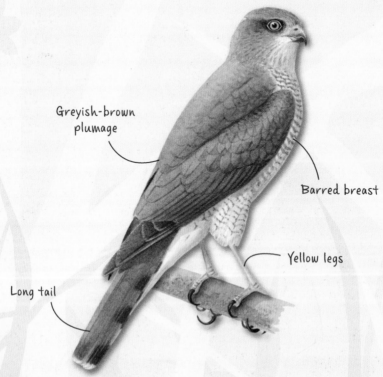

Greyish-brown plumage

Barred breast

Yellow legs

Long tail

KESTREL

Native birds of prey, kestrels are often spotted hovering above roadside verges. They perch on telegraph poles or tall trees nearby, looking out for opportunities to feed on prey, such as small mammals (especially voles), beetles, worms and small birds. Kestrels have extraordinary eyesight and can spot a beetle 50 m away. If they catch a number of voles in one day, they may hide the leftovers and eat them later on – usually as the sun is setting.

Kestrels were once common in British farms, but their numbers are in decline. This is probably due to the loss of their habitats, which has meant a shortage of food.

Back is spotted with black

Short, round head

Slim tail with a black band

PEREGRINE

Peregrine falcons are birds of prey that live throughout Europe. They can adapt to a wide range of habitats, as long as there is enough food to support them. Peregrines mostly feed on other birds, such as pigeons, which they catch in flight. They can see their prey at a great distance, then swoop in for the kill, reaching top speeds of 180 km/h. Once they have caught their prey, peregrines eat almost the entire body, leaving just the intestines and the breastbone.

FACT FILE

Scientific name
Falco peregrinus
Size 39–50 cm
Wingspan 100–120 cm
Call 'Kee-kee' or 'hak-kaak'
Breeding 2–4 eggs, one brood, from March to June

By the 1960s, 80 percent of the British peregrine population had died due to pesticide poisoning. The worst pesticides were banned and populations have grown.

Yellow eye-ring

Blue-grey plumage on back

White, speckled breast

Thin, grey bands on belly and sides

Yellow feet

COMMON PHEASANT

Introduced centuries ago from Asia as a game bird, most pheasants are reared in controlled areas for shooting. However, many also live outside the artificial breeding pens. The pheasant has adapted well to the European woodlands. When alarmed it usually runs from danger, crouching low to the ground. If it is approached too closely, the pheasant erupts into the air with a startling clatter of wings before flying and gliding to safety. A ground forager, the pheasant is often seen at the edge of woods, on farmland, and in parks and large gardens.

Due to unnaturally high numbers of birds bred for hunting, pheasants are frequent road casualties.

Red wattle

Speckled breast

Coppery coloured plumage

Long, barred-pattern tail

COOT

Coots are closely related to the moorhen. They can easily be told from their smaller cousins by their entirely black plumage with a white beak and 'shield' on the forehead, which gives us the phrase 'bald as a coot'. They live on lakes and reservoirs, where they gather in large numbers in winter. They feed on vegetation and invertebrates that they collect by diving down in deeper water.

FACT FILE

Scientific name *Fulica atra*

Size 35–40 cm

Wingspan 75 cm

Call Noisy, trumpeting 'keet'

Breeding 5–7 eggs, early summer

During winter, you may see the coot feeding alongside the gadwall. The coot dives down and brings up waterweed to feed on, which the gadwall then steals.

White beak and face shield

Black plumage

Red eye

Yellow legs

MOORHEN

The moorhen is a familiar bird, creeping nervously around the edge of park lakes or swimming jerkily across ponds and canals. They can be told apart from the similar coot by the large, white patches under the tail, a white line on their sides and the colour of their bill and forehead 'shield', which are red with a yellow tip. Moorhens feed on vegetation, seeds and invertebrates, including water snails.

FACT FILE

Scientific name
Gallinula chloropus

Size 25–30 cm

Wingspan 55 cm

Call Loud, high-pitched 'krrrrrk'

Breeding 5–7 eggs, during spring and summer

Moorhens have two broods of young each year. The young birds from the first brood will help their parents to look after the chicks from the second brood.

White patches

White line

Yellow legs

Red bill with yellow tip

AVOCET

Beautiful, elegant wading birds, avocets are found in coastal habitats, especially in eastern England. They have distinctive black-and-white plumage, long legs and an unusually long beak. They use their beak to sweep through mud, searching for insects, shelled animals and worms to eat. Avocets became extinct in Britain in the 19th century, but they were successfully reintroduced to England in the 1940s. Now they are the symbol for the RSPB (Royal Society for the Protection of Birds).

Chicks face a difficult few months after hatching and if the weather is bad many of them may die. Few avocets live beyond seven years of age, but one has lived to 24 years.

Black cap and hind neck

Long, black bill that curves upwards

Black bars on wings

White undersides

OYSTERCATCHER

The oystercatcher has a strong bill that it uses to break open shellfish, such as cockles and mussels. These distinctive, sturdy birds live in most British coastal regions throughout the year, and often form enormous flocks that make a raucous noise. They walk along the seashore or mudflats, head down, as they search for food to eat. When they live inland, oystercatchers rely on earthworms as a major source of food. Despite their name, oystercatchers do not appear to eat oysters.

FACT FILE

Scientific name
Haematopus ostralegus
Size 40–45 cm
Wingspan 80–85 cm
Call Loud 'kleep kleep'
Breeding 2–3 eggs, from
April to July

Oystercatchers compete for shellfish with fishermen, sometimes bringing them into conflict.

Black-and-white plumage

Bright-red eye

Long, bright-orange bill

White wing bands

Large, bulky body

Pale pink legs

LAPWING

Once widespread on farms, lapwings are becoming less common because of modern farming techniques. Their black-and-white plumage, striking crest and unusual wavering flight pattern make lapwings easy to identify. They often survive the winters living in large flocks, but the birds separate in spring to go to their breeding grounds. At this time, the males start to display to females by rolling, diving and zigzagging in flight.

FACT FILE

Scientific name
Vanellus vanellus
Size 28–31 cm
Wingspan 70–76 cm
Call 'Weet' or 'whee-er-ee'
Breeding 3–4 eggs, from March to April, young hatch 3–4 weeks later

Lapwings make their nests in hollows on the ground. They choose places where they have a good all-round view, so they can spot predators.

Dark green plumage on back

Black cap with crest

Short, dark bill

White underwing

BIRDS • Waders

GREY PLOVER

Increasing numbers of grey plovers are spending the winter in Britain. Most go to warmer climates, travelling as far as Africa, Australasia and South America, after spending spring and summer here from April onwards. They all breed in the Siberian tundra. In Britain the grey plover is found on coastal mudflats and shores, feeding on mussels and other shellfish as well as lugworms. The grey plover rarely moves inland in Britain, preferring to stay close to the shore. It usually moves in small groups, often mingling with other species, and calling noisily as it forages.

FACT FILE

Scientific name
Pluvialis squatarola
Size 27–30 cm
Wingspan 75–80 cm
Call 'Tlee-oo-ee'
Breeding Four eggs in a clutch

The grey plover can be seen running along the tideline on beaches, picking up insects as well as sea creatures.

Grey and white plumage

Short, thin black bill

Long black legs

RINGED PLOVER

The ringed plover is short and stocky, and its black facial and breast markings contrast dramatically with its white front. Together with its brown cap and back, this means it is well camouflaged against the pebbles of the shingle beaches where it often nests. The ringed plover is a stop-start feeder, running along the water's edge and stopping to bob down and capture food items on the beach, including insects, worms and crustaceans.

FACT FILE

Scientific name
Charadrius hiaticula

Size 18–20 cm

Wingspan 50–55 cm

Call 'Too-li'

Breeding Four eggs in a clutch

Like other shore birds, the ringed plover patters the mud with its feet to bring worms to the surface. It does not probe with its bill.

Black-and-white head with brown cap

Black-and-white breast

Orange legs

TURNSTONE

Turnstones that winter in Britain have bred in Canada and Greenland. The passage migrants passing through Britain in spring and autumn breed in Scandinavia and winter in Africa. Rocky coasts provide it with abundant supplies of winkles, mussels and limpets, as well as the fast-moving invertebrates flushed out from beneath stones and seaweed patches. Sometimes several turnstones co-operate to overturn a heavy stone that one bird cannot manage alone.

FACT FILE

Scientific name
Arenaria interpres
Size 21–25 cm
Wingspan 50–55 cm
Call 'Tuk-a-tuk' and 'kyug'
Breeding Four eggs in a clutch

The turnstone has earned its name from the way it overturns stones, moves seaweed and digs sand to catch the tiny creatures that scatter as they are exposed.

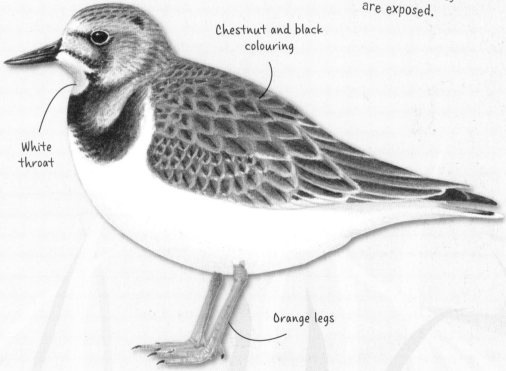

Chestnut and black colouring

White throat

Orange legs

SANDERLING

The sanderling is always on the move, usually running. On the ground, flocks of sanderlings run like streams of insects as they hurry and bustle in their continual quest for worms, shellfish and shrimps. In the air, flocks fly in co-ordinated movement over mudflats. The sanderling breeds in the high Arctic regions of Canada, Greenland, Scandinavia and Siberia. It migrates in winter as far south as Australasia, though some winter much further north, including those that are seen in Britain.

Sanderlings like to feed right at the edge of the water where the waves break. They scurry towards the retreating water to pick up morsels, then run back up the beach as the waves return.

Black and white tail

Short, straight black bill

White breast

KNOT

The knot is a sociable, small wader. It is usually seen in large flocks on mudflats and sandy estuaries in winter in Britain, mainly on east and northwest coasts. It breeds in the Arctic regions of Europe, North America and Asia. The close-packed flocks of knots cover the feeding-ground like a moving carpet, all probing rapidly for food. Occasionally they take to the air to perform complicated formation aerobatics, all turning and wheeling at exactly the same time. They feed on small shellfish such as cockles and immature mussels.

FACT FILE

Scientific name
Calidris canutus
Size 25 cm
Wingspan 55–60 m
Call 'Nutt' and whistling 'twit-twit'
Breeding Four eggs in a clutch

A flock may contain many thousands of birds.

Eye-stripe

Grey back

Short, straight bill

Dark green legs

DUNLIN

The dunlin visits the British Isles in huge numbers for the winter, and is the nation's commonest wader. Dunlins run and quarrel as they probe beneath the surface of estuary mud and coastal sand for snails and ragworms. The large flocks fly in close formation, and will suddenly take off from the feeding-site in unison, make a wheeling circuit, then land again to resume feeding. Those that breed in Britain arrive in April, sometimes establishing nest-sites at altitudes of up to 1000 m in Scotland.

FACT FILE

Scientific name *Calidris alpina*

Size 16–19 cm

Wingspan 40 cm

Call Harsh 'treer''

Breeding Four eggs in a clutch

At a distance, a close-packed flock of dunlins looks like moving smoke as they wheel and sweep over their feeding-grounds.

Grey crown

Black and white tail

White belly

REDSHANK

The redshank breeds throughout the British Isles, nesting in marshes, moorlands and meadows. Outside the breeding season it moves to coastal flatlands and estuaries. Here it swims and wades as it probes the mud for molluscs, worms, crustaceans and insects. The male has a spectacular courting dance, approaching the female with wings raised to display the white under-surfaces, and performing a slow, high-stepping walk with his long red legs. He then begins to flutter his wings, leaving the ground entirely with each step, trilling noisily.

The redshank is a noisy bird, emitting loud alarm calls when intruders approach its nest. It does this both from perches, such as fence posts, and while flying.

Greyish-brown upper parts with dark streaks

Red legs

Dark brown bill with red base

BAR-TAILED GODWIT

Rarely seen inland, the bar-tailed godwit wades through the shallows on its long legs, probing the tidal mud and sandbanks of estuaries for food with its long bill. It is a sociable bird that is usually seen in company with other waders, such as knots, redshanks, oystercatchers and curlews, at the water's edge. The bar-tailed godwit feeds on worms, shellfish, crustaceans, water larvae and all sorts of insects. It is found in sandier areas than its relative, the black-tailed godwit, especially those rich in lugworms.

FACT FILE

Scientific name
Limosa lapponica
Size 41 cm
Wingspan 75 cm
Call 'Ved-ved-ved' in flight.
Also 'kirruc-kirruc'
Breeding Four eggs in a clutch

When the godwit sees a coiled worm-cast appearing on the surface, it quickly plunges its beak deep into the sand before the lugworm can burrow out of reach.

Long, thin bill with pink base

Reddish-brown breast

Long black legs

CURLEW

Some curlews live permanently in Britain, and can be spotted in coastal areas and other watery habitats throughout the year. Others spend the winter here, and return to Scandinavia when spring arrives. These waders are famous for their beautiful spring song, which has been described as eerie and can be heard at night as well as in the day. Curlews often gather together in large numbers to feed, particularly at the mud flats on estuaries.

Curlews use their unusually long, slender bills to probe the soft mud in search of small animals to eat, such as worms, starfish, crabs and other shelled animals.

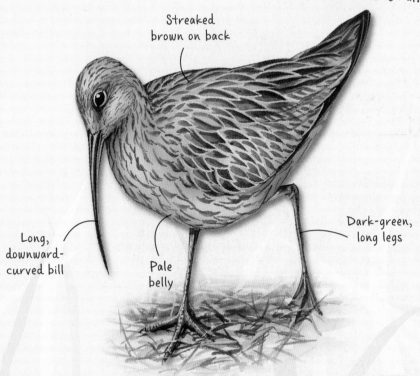

Streaked brown on back

Long, downward-curved bill

Pale belly

Dark-green, long legs

ARCTIC SKUA

The fast and acrobatic Arctic skua relentlessly chases puffins, kittiwakes and terns. The skua makes them bring up fish they have eaten, which it then catches and eats in midair. During the chase it sprints and turns like a hawk. Its normal flight is steady and graceful. The colony usually posts two or three sentry birds to give the alarm when predators or other intruders approach. As well as fish, the Arctic skua kills and eats adult and young birds, and will also feed on carrion.

FACT FILE

Scientific name
Stercorarius parasiticus
Size 41–46 cm
Wingspan 118 cm
Call Wails, barks and a squealing 'eee-air'
Breeding Two eggs in a clutch

When protecting its nest and young, it will attack anything from sheep to humans.

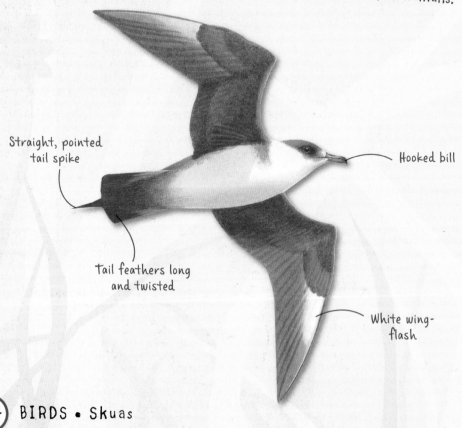

Straight, pointed tail spike

Hooked bill

Tail feathers long and twisted

White wing-flash

GREAT SKUA

The bulky great skua chases birds to steal their meals as other skuas do, but goes for large prey, such as gannets, gulls and ducks. In the summer it also kills and eats other sea birds. It brings down its prey by dive-bombing it from a great height. Once almost extinct in the British Isles, the great skua has made a comeback, and is a regular summer resident in northern sites in the Orkney and Shetland islands. It is rarely seen inland in winter.

FACT FILE

Scientific name
Stercorarius skua

Size 53–58 cm

Wingspan 135–140 cm

Call Harsh 'skeerr', also 'tuh-tuh' when attacking

Breeding Two eggs in a clutch

The great skua makes alarming attacks on intruders to its nest-sites, swooping down in a steep dive and striking with its feet as it sweeps past.

White wing-flash

Brown speckled plumage

Blunt tail

Powerful build

BLACK-HEADED GULL

One of the commonest British gulls, the black-headed gull is now found inland, both feeding and breeding, as often as on the shore. In its coastal habitat of low shores, harbours and estuaries, fish is an important part of its diet. However, its increased presence inland owes much to its enthusiasm for rubbish dumps and the worms that surface from playing fields. Inland black-headed gulls feed on insects, worms and snails as well as waste scraps and carrion.

FACT FILE

Scientific name
Larus ridibundus
Size 35–38 cm
Wingspan 105 cm
Call Harsh 'skeerr', also 'tuh-tuh' when attacking
Breeding 2–3 eggs in a clutch

Black-headed gulls are often seen following ploughs. They are fond of swimming, and outside the breeding season, sometimes come into riverside cities.

Incomplete eye-ring

Red bill

Blue-grey wings

Black wing-tips

Long, red legs

MEDITERRANEAN GULL

Rare in Britain, but increasing in numbers, the Mediterranean gull can sometimes be found around western and southern coasts in marshes and coastal flat lands. Closely related to the British black-headed gull, the Mediterranean gull is a bulkier bird, with a heavier bill and longer legs. It feeds mainly on insects, crabs and small fish. It usually breeds in the Balkans and southeastern Europe, but up to 50 pairs now breed annually in the British Isles, in salt marshes and tidal mud flats.

FACT FILE

Scientific name
Larus melanocephalus

Size 36–38 cm

Wingspan 96 cm

Call 'Keeow' and 'ayeeah'.
When alarmed ga-ga-ga'.

Breeding Three eggs in a clutch

This gull may fly great distances from the colony to feed on grasslands, and also likes to feed at the edge of the sea close to breaking waves.

Broken white eye-ring

Winter plumage

Pale grey wings

Red legs

COMMON GULL

Far less common in England and Wales than its name suggests, the common gull is more numerous in Scotland, particularly in the north and the islands. It is a good swimmer and diver, and will submerge entirely in pursuit of fish. It is increasingly seen inland, usually in farming areas, and also around reservoirs and lakes. It is a scavenger that will eat most things, including bird eggs. Common gulls are social birds, and will gang up on a predator such as a hawk or a skua threatening the community.

FACT FILE

Scientific name *Larus canus*

Size 40–42 cm

Wingspan 120 cm

Call High, shrill, squealing yelps and chattering cries

Breeding Three eggs in a clutch

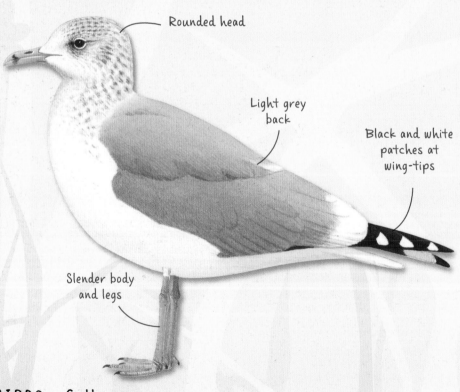

Rounded head

Light grey back

Black and white patches at wing-tips

Slender body and legs

KITTIWAKE

The kittiwake usually fishes on the surface of the sea, and never scavenges the tideline like other gulls. It feeds on fish, crustaceans, worms and trawler waste. The kittiwake is the smallest of the gulls breeding in the British Isles. It spends winter at sea, and spring and summer on some of the most inaccessible and sheer cliff ledge nest-sites in the country. In flight the kittiwake is graceful, and it moves faster than larger gulls, using rapid wing-beats. It dives like a tern from the air when fishing, and uses its wings to swim under water.

FACT FILE

Scientific name
Rissa tridactyla

Size 38–41 cm

Wingspan 105–110 cm

Call 'Kitti-way-ake'

Breeding Two eggs in a clutch

Grey back

Black wing-tips

White underparts

HERRING GULL

The most widespread of all British coastal birds, the herring gull is well known to holidaymakers at seaside towns and beaches. These large birds have little fear of humans and will approach them for food. They also have other ways of feeding, such as trampling on mud to make worms come to the surface and scouring rubbish tips looking for morsels to eat. Herring gulls have even been seen to drop crabs and other shellfish on rocks or roads to break them open.

FACT FILE

Scientific name
Larus argentatus
Size 55–67 cm
Wingspan 130–160 cm
Call Loud 'kyow', 'ga-ga-ga'
Breeding 2–3 eggs, in May

Herring gulls are omnivores. This means that they can eat a wide range of food. They often follow fishing boats for miles, waiting for fish scraps to be thrown overboard.

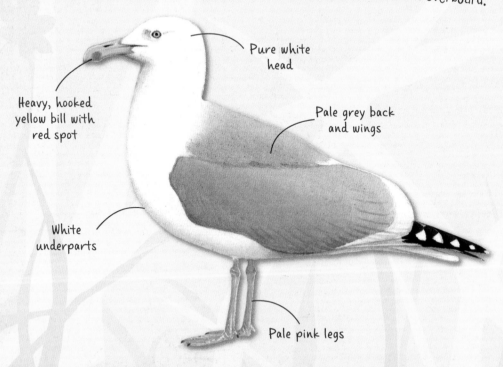

Pure white head

Heavy, hooked yellow bill with red spot

Pale grey back and wings

White underparts

Pale pink legs

LESSER BLACK-BACKED GULL

A bird of islands, moors and cliff-tops, the lesser black-backed gull is a fierce predator of other seabirds, as well as of their eggs and young. It follows fishing boats and other vessels far out to sea, much farther than most other birds, often for many hours at a time. It also scavenges at harbours and dumps. The chicks leave the nest a few days after hatching, and forage on the ground, guarded by their parents for at least six weeks.

FACT FILE

Scientific name *Larus fuscus*

Size 50–52 cm

Wingspan 142 cm

Call Loud, deep 'ow-ow-ow-kyow'

Breeding Three eggs in a clutch

This gull is very protective of its nest and young, and a whole colony will take to the air to drive off intruders.

Thick bill shape

All dark upperparts

Yellow legs

White marks on wing-tips

GLAUCOUS GULL

The large glaucous gull is fairly rare in Britain. It visits in winter from its Arctic breeding-grounds, and is most often seen in groups of mixed gulls. They appear inland on reservoirs and scavenging in rubbish tips. The glaucous gull is fond of crabs and shellfish, and hangs around fish docks with other gulls, on the look-out for fish scraps. It is a bold bird, and feared by smaller gulls, but is not as aggressive as the greater black-backed gull. As well as eating animal food, it is known to feed on plants, including seaweed and berries.

FACT FILE

Scientific name
Larus hyperboreus

Size 52–68 cm

Wingspan 158 cm

Call Occasional 'eeee-yoch-yoch-yoch' and 'kak-ak-ak'

Breeding Three eggs in a clutch

It takes other birds' eggs, and will also catch small mammals if given the chance.

Red spot on bill

White wing-tips

Pink legs

GREAT BLACK-BACKED GULL

The great black-backed gull is an imposing bird, dramatically coloured, bulky and equipped with a powerful beak. It usually lives around rocky coasts and cliffs, though it is increasingly found in estuaries, and inland at reservoirs, rubbish tips and fields. It is a fearsome predator as well as a scavenger. It can gulp down a whole rabbit, and will attack flocks of water birds in search of a meal. It also hangs around docks and fishing boats, especially in winter. It feeds on carrion when it gets the chance, and one of its local names is corpse-eater.

FACT FILE

Scientific name
Larus marinus
Size 62–65 cm
Wingspan 158 cm
Call Deep-pitched 'owk-uk-uk-uk'. Also wails and squeals
Breeding 2–3 eggs in a clutch

The great black-backed gull can soar to great heights, and also skims the waves, like an albatross.

Large head and bill

Black back

White breast

ARCTIC TERN

The Arctic tern travels farther than any other bird. It breeds mainly in the Arctic, and winters at sea in the Antarctic. When migrating, it flies close to the sea surface, sometimes resting on floating objects. It likes to breed on rocky offshore islands, and can be seen nesting in large and small colonies around Scottish and Irish coasts, particularly in Shetland and Orkney. Sometimes known as the sea swallow, this graceful bird returns to the same nest each year.

FACT FILE

Scientific name
Sterna paradisaea

Size 80–110 cm

Wingspan 80 cm

Call 'Kee-arrr' and 'kee-kee'

Breeding 1–2 eggs in a clutch

The Arctic tern fearlessly attacks all intruders at its nest-sites, and birdwatchers have even needed medical treatment after a mass attack.

Wing looks translucent

Long, white, forked tail

Red bill

COMMON TERN

The common tern is often seen over rivers, hovering and swooping as it feeds. Elegant, but aggressive, this bird is seen across Britain in summer. During the autumn it migrates to warmer climates, returning in spring. It nests in noisy colonies and flies out to sea in search of food. Common terns are light and graceful in flight and can travel for many kilometres before tiring and returning to land. When they spot fish below them, terns plunge-dive into the water in pursuit of their prey.

FACT FILE

Scientific name *Sterna hirundo*

Size 32–33 cm

Wingspan 82–95 cm

Call 'Kreee-yar' or 'kik kik keer'

Breeding Up to four eggs are laid around May, hatching about three weeks later

These birds have long bodies and are elegant in flight. On land, however, they move awkwardly, because of their short legs.

Pale underwing with dark band at back edge

Grey back

Black cap

Bright-red bill with a black tip

Long, forked tail

LITTLE TERN

The little tern is tiny compared to the other British terns. It nests on shingle ridges and sandy beaches, which brings it into conflict with holidaymakers. Like other terns it hovers and dives when fishing, and uses very fast wing beats, which give it a flickering flight. The little tern can often be seen fishing right above the waves as they break on the beach. It dives for surface fish, but also catches insects on the wing.

FACT FILE

Scientific name *Sterna albifrons*

Size 50–60 cm

Wingspan 52 cm

Call Fast 'kirri-ki-ki' and 'kyik'.

Breeding 2–3 eggs in a clutch

The breeding colonies are small, and these birds fly around intruders repeating a 'duip' alarm call, then fall back until the coast is clear.

Black wing-tips

White forehead

Yellow bill with black tip

SANDWICH TERN

This is the largest of the terns visiting the British Isles. It is the first to arrive in the spring, and many pairs breed on shingle beaches, in coastal dunes and around some inland waters. The noise of a large colony can be heard a considerable distance away. The sandwich tern likes being in large groups, and often mixes with other terns. It is also less aggressive towards intruders. It still swoops down but does not strike. It lives on sand-eels, fish and molluscs. Once the young have left the nest, they may be fed by any of the adults in the group.

FACT FILE

Scientific name
Sterna sandvicensis

Size 36–38 cm

Wingspan 100 cm

Call Loud 'kirrik' and 'kik'

Breeding 1–2 eggs in a clutch

The tern dives from a greater height than most terns when fishing and disappears entirely under the water.

Black crown

Short forked tail

Long black bill with yellow tip

White breast

GUILLEMOT

The guillemot spends much of its life at sea, coming ashore to breed in packed colonies on cliff ledges and on the flat tops of offshore rock stacks. Groups of guillemots fly up to 50 km to their feeding-grounds each day. Their relatively short wings have a fast, whirring beat as they skim low over the water. About three weeks after hatching, the guillemot chick leaps down from the cliffs to the water or rocks below, where it is joined by the male parent, which leads it out to sea.

FACT FILE

Scientific name *Uria alge*

Size 38–41 cm

Wingspan 65–70 cm

Call Extended 'aarrgh'

Breeding One egg in a clutch

The guillemot is a strong and expert swimmer, diving as deep as 50 m in pursuit of fish.

White underparts

Blackish-brown plumage

Short, rounded tail

RAZORBILL

Half the world's population of razorbills breeds in Britain and Ireland. When feeding its young, it can carry up to a dozen small fish at a time in its large beak. Razorbills start to come ashore near the breeding-site in February, but do not begin nesting and breeding until March or later. They begin to leave the site again in July. They spend the entire winter at sea, unless driven ashore by particularly strong storms. British breeding birds migrate as far as the Mediterranean in winter.

FACT FILE

Scientific name *Alca torda*

Size 40 cm

Wingspan 66 cm

Call A grating 'grrr' in the colony

Breeding One egg in a clutch

The razorbill is ungainly on land, and walks with a shuffle, but is perfectly at home in the sea, where it is an excellent swimmer.

Black bill with white vertical line

Small, pointed tail

White breast

BLACK GUILLEMOT

The black guillemot is about the size of a pigeon, and nests in small groups, not gathering like the guillemot in huge colonies. It flies fast and low, and can swim expertly underwater, catching small fish and seabed creatures such as worms and molluscs. It is found around the coasts of Ireland and north and west Scotland, in Anglesey in Wales and Cumbria in England. It tends to stay closer to land than other guillemots, fishing in shallow waters. It winters at sea, not too far from its breeding territories, and returns each year to the same nest-site.

FACT FILE

Scientific name *Cepphus grylle*
Size 30–32 cm
Wingspan 55 cm
Call High-pitched whistles and whines, 'dinsie-dinsie'
Breeding 1–2 eggs in a clutch

When threatening intruders it opens its beak very wide to reveal the bright red interior.

All black summer plumage

Black bill

White wing-patch

PUFFIN

The puffin is an unmistakable sea bird with its black crown, colourful summer bill and clown-like white face. Puffins breed in large colonies in Britain and Ireland. They are skilled divers, and can swim to depths of 15 m to catch several fish at a time without surfacing. They build their nests in burrows that they dig themselves, or they use old rabbit burrows. Puffins have large, strong feet that they use as air-brakes when landing, as well as for swimming and digging.

FACT FILE

Scientific name
Fratercula arctica
Size 26–29 cm
Wingspan 47–63 cm
Call Loud 'aar' or 'kar-ooo-ar'
Breeding One egg, May to June, adults stay in the breeding area until August

When young puffins leave the nest they head for the sea, following the light. Sometimes they are confused by nearby bright city lights, and head inland instead.

Dark eye

White face

Large, colourful, triangular bill

Black plumage on upper parts

Short tail

Large, orangey-red feet

WOODPIGEON

The largest of all European pigeons, woodpigeons are commonly seen in gardens, parks, woodlands and around farms. Their feathers are mostly grey with a pinkish breast. As they have unusually dense, heavy feathers, they often appear almost round. These birds can be recognized when they walk by their distinctive waddle. Pigeons often eat seeds, but they will eat almost anything on a bird table.

Most birds drink water by gulping it, then throwing their heads back, so the water pours down their throats. However pigeons suck water, using their beaks like straws.

Bright yellow eye

White-and-green bars on neck

Grey plumage on upperparts

Plump body

Narrow white bar visible on edge of wing

Short, red legs

ROCK DOVE

The rock dove is the ancestor of all domestic pigeons. These were originally bred from wild birds for eating and for racing. The feral pigeons seen in both town and country are descendants of domestic escapees. In its natural state, the rock dove lives among the rocks and cliffs of coasts and islands. It feeds on seeds and plant material in fields and woods, and perches on rocks or on the ground in preference to trees.

FACT FILE

Scientific name
Columba livia

Size 31–34 cm

Wingspan 64–72 cm

Call 'Ruh-ruh-ruh'

Breeding Two eggs in spring, can breed throughout the year

Very few pure rock doves have survived in most parts of the country, due to interbreeding with feral relatives.

Black-and-white bill

Double black wing-bars

Metallic-looking neck pattern

White underwings and rump

STOCK DOVE

More solitary than woodpigeons, stock doves can sometimes be seen feeding alongside them in winter. Found everywhere in Britain except the extreme north of Scotland, the stock dove's habitats include woods, rocky coasts, dunes, cliffs and parkland. It occasionally eats snails and larvae, but most of its food is vegetable, including leaves, crops such as beans and corn, clover, seeds, buds and flowers.

FACT FILE

Scientific name *Columba oenas*

Size 32–34 cm

Wingspan 63–69 cm

Call 'OOO-roo-oo'

Breeding Two eggs, 2–3 broods all year

The stock dove has an impressive display in the breeding season. Both males and females fly around in circles, gliding with raised wings, and 'clapping' their wings.

Glossy, turquoise-green neck

Small wing-bars

Broad tail band

COLLARED DOVE

The collared dove has become common in Britain only in the last **50 years.** This bird stays close to human society. It feeds alongside farm poultry and cattle, sharing their meals, and also hangs around docks, breweries, stables and zoos, where there is grain to be found. It is seen in both towns and villages, and soon locates local bird tables, turning up regularly for seeds and scraps.

FACT FILE

Scientific name
Streptopelia decaocto
Size 28–32 cm
Wingspan 47–55 cm
Call Deep 'coo-coooo, coo',
'hwee' in flight
Breeding Two eggs,
2–3 broods all year

Where food is plentiful, the collared dove may feed in sizable flocks, especially in winter. It eats snails and insects as well as seeds.

Narrow, black half-collar

Pinkish breast

Fawny grey wings

White undertail

TURTLE DOVE

Named after its soft, purring 'turr turr' call, the turtle dove is about **26 cm in length.** This slim, fast-flying dove is smaller than a woodpigeon and has different markings to a collared dove. In late summer, turtle doves often perch on bushes and wires in small groups. Their nests are platforms of twigs built in trees or thorny bushes. Although they spend winter in Africa, they breed in the UK during summer.

FACT FILE

Scientific name
Streptopelia turtur
Size 26 cm
Wingspan 49–55 cm
Call Cackling 'ag-ag-ag-arrr'
Breeding Two eggs, two broods
a year, from May

The population of turtle doves is falling quickly and the species is now on the 'red list'.

Greyish head

Black-and-white bars on neck

Mottled black-and-brown back

Pinkish breast

Long tail with narrow tip

CUCKOO

The cuckoo is known for its very distinctive call, and is often thought to be the harbinger of spring. The female watches a pair of small birds building their nest and at the moment they are absent will visit it, remove one of their eggs and lay her own single egg in its place. The unsuspecting small birds find themselves the parents to a huge and hungry cuckoo chick. Cuckoos are a widespread summer visitor in the British Isles.

FACT FILE

Scientific name
Cuculus canorus
Size 30–33 cm
Wingspan 71–76 cm
Call 'Coo-cooo' from male, chuckling bubbling call from female
Breeding 25 eggs in a season

During courtship, males spread their tail feathers, droop their wings and swivel their body round.

Grey back and head

Pointed wings

Long tail

TAWNY OWL

The tawny owl is a woodland predator that also lives in parks and gardens. These nocturnal birds normally hunt for small mammals, but they have moved into urban areas in search of small birds that gather around bird tables. Like other owls, they fly in eerie silence, their wing beats muffled by the downy edges of their wing feathers. As well as mammals and birds, tawny owls feed on insects, newts, frogs and bats.

FACT FILE

Scientific name *Strix aluco*

Size 37–39 cm

Wingspan 94–104 cm

Call Hooting 'hoo-hoo' or 'ke-wik'

Breeding 2–5 eggs, one brood, from April to June

Tawny owls can look behind by twisting their heads around. They can pinpoint sound accurately by moving their heads to get a 'fix' on the source of the noise.

Mottled, brown feathers

Large, round head with distinctive facial disc and dark eyes

Paler colouring on underside

BARN OWL

Barn owls hunt for their food at **night.** Their bodies are covered in white-and-golden feathers. Like other owls, their eyes are on the front of their head. They prefer open areas of land, but can be seen flying over gardens in the late evening as they search for prey. Barn owls make their homes in sheds, church spires and natural holes in trees.

Barn owls live alone or in pairs. Males and females usually mate for life and both parents look after the chicks. They are rare, and their nests must not be disturbed.

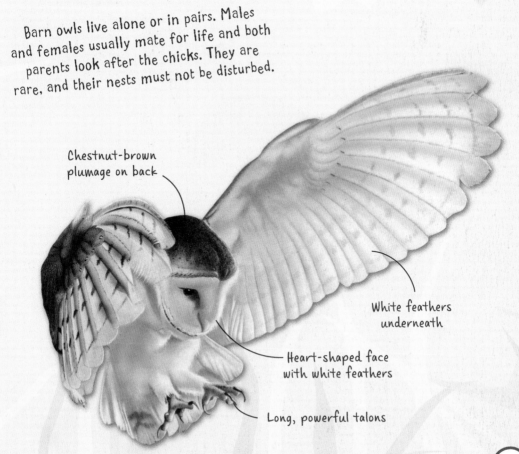

Chestnut-brown plumage on back

White feathers underneath

Heart-shaped face with white feathers

Long, powerful talons

KINGFISHER

Kingfishers live near slow-moving shallow waterways, where they can hunt for small fish, especially minnows and sticklebacks. They favour places with trees that overhang the water, as they provide perfect perching posts where the birds can wait patiently, watching for prey. As it dives into the water, a kingfisher opens its bill, closes its eyes and catches the fish. It returns to the perch, where it kills the fish by smashing it against the branch.

FACT FILE

Scientific name *Alcedo atthis*

Size 16–17 cm

Wingspan 24–26 cm

Call Loud, sharp 'kit-chee'

Breeding 5–7 eggs, two broods a year, in May and July

Kingfishers have their own territories, or hunting grounds. A territory may be a 1–5 km stretch of water that the bird has to defend.

Barred, blue cap

Long, pointed black bill

White-and-orange cheek patch

Bright, electric-blue plumage on back

Rusty orange feathers on underside

GREEN WOODPECKER

The handsome green woodpecker lives in woodlands and parklands, and is Britain's largest woodpecker. It uses its long, pointed beak to excavate its nest hole and to dig for ants, its main food. The ants stick to the woodpecker's long, sticky tongue. In the garden, these birds are more likely to drill the lawn for ants than approach the bird table. When ants' nests are frozen, woodpeckers have been known to bore into beehives.

FACT FILE

Scientific name *Picus viridis*

Size 30–33 cm

Wingspan 40–42 cm

Call Loud, laughing 'gluck-gluck-gluck'

Breeding 5–7 eggs, one brood, May to July

Green woodpeckers are shy but noisy birds, and are unmistakable with their bold colouring. Also unmistakable is its loud cry, resembling hysterical laughter.

Crimson-red crown and nape

Black-and-red moustache

Bright green upperparts

Green-grey underparts

GREAT SPOTTED WOODPECKER

Boldly coloured, the great spotted woodpecker is black and white with red under its tail. Males also have a red splash on the nape of their neck. Youngsters look similar, but their colours are less bold. These birds are about the size of a blackbird. They live in woodlands, parks and gardens with large trees, and scurry across tree trunks looking for insects to eat.

FACT FILE

Scientific name
Dendrocopos major

Size 22–33 cm

Wingspan 34–42 cm

Call Sharp, short 'tchak'

Breeding 4–7 white eggs, from April to June

Woodpeckers make a characteristic drumming noise with their beaks on trees. They look for bugs in the cracks in bark, and have very long tongues for picking up food.

Pointed beak

Red nape of neck

White wing patches

Red under the tail

LESSER SPOTTED WOODPECKER

The lesser spotted woodpecker is about the size of a sparrow. Its colouring is like the greater spotted woodpecker's, but arranged differently. It is a shy bird, hunting insects out of sight in high branches. Lesser spotted woodpeckers drum on tree trunks to mark their territory. They are rarely seen at the bird table, approaching it nervously, if at all. These birds are usually only seen in England and Wales.

FACT FILE

Scientific name
Dendrocopus minor
Size 13–14 cm
Wingspan 25–27 cm
Call 'Kee-kee-kee', weak 'tchik'
Breeding 4–6 eggs, one brood, May to July

Unlike other woodpeckers, lesser spotted woodpeckers join winter feeding flocks of mixed tits.

Bright red crown

Black-and-white feathers

Short, thin, grey bill

SWIFT

Swifts are extraordinary birds and superb flyers. They rarely come to land and spend almost all of their lives in the air, even sleeping while in flight. Once fledglings leave the nest, they may remain airborne for the next two or three years, until they reach breeding age. Swifts feed on insects and spiders that they catch in mid-air. They arrive in Britain in April, for the breeding season, and often nest in the eaves of old buildings. They leave in July or August.

FACT FILE

Scientific name *Apus apus*

Size 16–17 cm

Wingspan 42–48 cm

Call Loud screeches and screams

Breeding 2–3 eggs, from May to June

British swifts spend the winter in Africa, where they follow the rains. After rainfall, insect populations boom, providing a good food supply for these birds.

Plumage is black-brown all over

Long, narrow wings

Deeply forked, short tail

SHORE LARK

A rare winter visitor, the shore lark usually turns up on Britain's eastern and southeastern coasts in late autumn. There it can find the shingle, sand and salt marshes, which are its preferred winter habitat after breeding in the dry tundras of northern Scandinavia. Some shore larks stay in Britain for winter, but others pass through on the way to other parts of Europe. The shore lark is a sociable bird, sometimes seen in company with snow buntings and Lapland buntings.

FACT FILE

Scientific name
Eremophila alpestris

Size 16.5 cm

Wingspan 34–42 cm

Call 'Tsee'; in flight 'tsee-di-diu'

Breeding 4–7 white eggs, from April to June

The shore lark's winter and summer diets are completely different. It lives on seeds, buds and insects when breeding, then switches to shellfish and crustaceans from the water's edge in winter.

'Horns' of black feathers

Black crest

Short black legs

SWALLOW

Difficult to identify because they are rarely seen near the ground, swallows are extremely agile flyers. They can be seen swooping through the air as they hunt for insects to eat. Their wings are long and pointed, and their tails are deeply forked, unlike swifts and house martins. Swallows migrate to Europe from Africa in spring. Fewer swallows are coming to the UK than previously, but the reason for this is unknown.

FACT FILE

Scientific name *Hirundo rustica*

Size 17–22 cm

Wingspan 30–35 cm

Call Rapid twitter

Breeding 4–5 eggs with white spots, from April to August

Farmers avoid destroying swallow nests because the birds are thought to bring good luck. Swallows use second-hand nests — some are more than 50 years old.

Tail measures up to 7 cm in length and is deeply forked

Wings are long and pointed

Dark blue feathers on back and wings

Pale cream feathers underneath

Distinctive red throat and face

HOUSE MARTIN

Often mistaken for swallows, house martins are actually smaller, have shorter tail forks and a white chin. They feed on flying insects, swooping over water or farmland to catch their prey. House martins are rarely seen on land, although they may be spotted over the garden at dusk. They often live in gardens with muddy pools, as they make their nests from mud. House martins migrate to hot countries in October, returning in spring.

FACT FILE

Scientific name *Delichon urbica*

Size 12–15 cm

Wingspan 25–30 cm

Call Twittering

Breeding 4–5 white eggs, from May to August

House martins are occasionally attracted to hot–air balloons. They fly in circles above the balloons, maybe enjoying a free ride on the rising current of warm air.

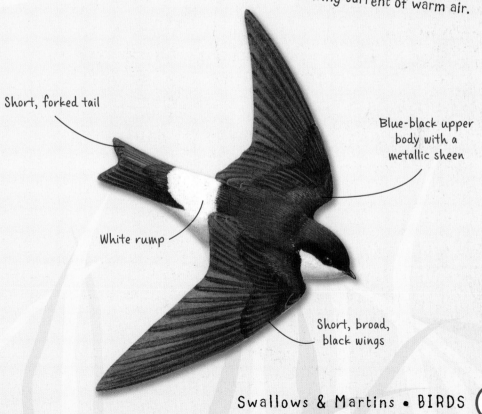

Short, forked tail

White rump

Blue-black upper body with a metallic sheen

Short, broad, black wings

PIED WAGTAIL

Pied wagtails visit gardens, parks and open fields, often near water. They are comical birds, often seen running quickly, pausing only to look at the ground and wag their tails up and down. Although the plumage of pied wagtails is black and white, the actual patterns and depth of colour varies over the year. Females have more grey than black feathers. Pied wagtails usually eat insects.

FACT FILE

Scientific name *Motacilla alba*

Size 17–20 cm

Wingspan 25–30 cm

Call Twittering song

Breeding 4–6 white eggs with grey spots, from April to June

These birds are often mistaken for young magpies, but they can be distinguished by their wagging tails.

Black crown, throat and upper breast

White face and black eye

White bars on wing feathers

Long tail that constantly moves

White feathers

ROCK PIPIT

Rock pipits are hard to see as they forage among coastal rocks and seaweed, feeding on tiny molluscs. Their dark colouring is a good camouflage among the rocks and vegetation, and they are often only noticed when they take to the air, flitting erratically between rocks and along the shore. Rock pipits are found around most of the coastline except for stretches without rocky shores.

FACT FILE

Scientific name
Anthus petrosus
Size 21–30 cm
Wingspan 20–25 cm
Call 'Peep-peep' alarm call
Breeding 4–5 eggs, from April to June

The rock pipit's calls and song are particularly loud, as it has to compete with the general noise of waves crashing on a rocky shore.

Streaky patterning

Black tail with grey outer feathers

Dark legs

WREN

O ne of the smallest birds that visit gardens, wrens are small, stocky, restless birds. They can be seen rushing around, under trees or bushes where they are well camouflaged. Wrens have brown backs and brown-and-cream eye-stripes. Their pert tails are constantly moving. They use grass and leaves to build their globe-shaped nests in bushes, trees and holes in walls. The nests are lined with feathers.

FACT FILE

Scientific name
Troglodytes troglodytes

Size 9–10 cm

Wingspan 13–17 cm

Call Loud trills and warbling

Breeding 5–8 white eggs with reddish spots, from April to July

Wrens can travel many kilometres in search of food, or to find habitats that are sheltered from harsh weather.

Plumage is reddish brown on back, with faint black bars

Short, upright tail

Faint eye-stripe

Beak is very narrow and tip points slightly downwards

Pale feathers underneath

DUNNOCK

Dunnocks are sometimes called hedge sparrows because at first glance they look very similar to the house sparrow. However, a dunnock's beak is much slimmer than a sparrow's, because it feeds on insects rather than seeds (stouter beaks are better at cracking seeds open). Male and female dunnocks look similar with brown streaking and pink legs, although the females are a little duller.

Cuckoos lay eggs in dunnock nests. The dunnocks are unaware that they are incubating an intruder. After hatching, the cuckoo fledgling throws the dunnock chicks out of the nest.

Thin, sharp beak

Speckled feathers on back

Blue-grey throat, breast and eye-stripe

Pink legs

ROBIN

One of the most easily recognized garden birds, robins are dainty, with plump bodies and red breasts. They are known as gardeners' friends as they often perch nearby when soil is being dug over, and quickly leap on any insects that are exposed. Males and females look similar. Robins are associated with holly berries, not only because of Christmas, but also because in winter, when food is scarce, robins feed on the berries.

FACT FILE

Scientific name
Erithacus rubecula
Size 12–15 cm
Wingspan 20–22 cm
Call Warbling song
Breeding 5–6 white eggs, speckled with red, from March to July

Robins do not migrate from the UK, but in winter, robins from colder countries often migrate to the UK. These birds have paler breasts and are less tame.

Brown beak

Red breast

Brown plumage on back and wings

White feathers underneath

Brown legs

NIGHTINGALE

The nightingale is famously known for its beautiful, melodic song. It is commonly heard after dark but also frequently during the daytime. It is an unobtrusive reddish-brown bird with a longish, rounded tail that it spreads in song display. The nightingale is not an easy bird to observe as it inhabits areas of dense thicket and scrub vegetation, but the male can often be spotted perching openly to sing. Nightingales are most likely to be seen in southeast England.

FACT FILE

Scientific name
Luscinia megarhynchos
Size 17–24 cm
Wingspan 20–22 cm
Call Melodious song of trills, harsh 'tchak' and 'whooeet'
Breeding 4–5 eggs, from April to June

The nightingale often stands in an upright pose with its tail cocked to one side.

Red-brown upper feathers

Long, reddish tail

White throat and underbelly

SONG THRUSH

Often seen darting around between bushes, song thrushes use their ears and eyes to search for small insects or worms to eat. They have brown backs and pale, creamy-white speckled chests. Males and females look similar. Song thrushes live in woodlands, gardens and fields. They nest in trees, bushes and garden sheds.

Thrushes build cup-shaped nests from grasses and twigs. The inside is lined with mud and rotting wood, and is stuck together with saliva.

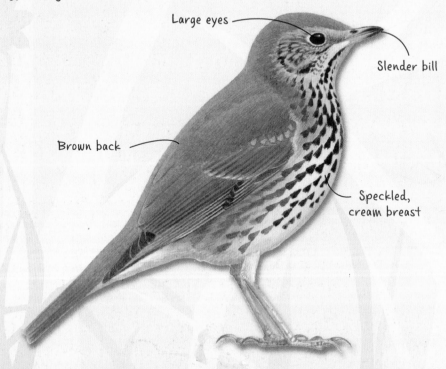

Large eyes

Slender bill

Brown back

Speckled, cream breast

MISTLE THRUSH

The mistle thrush is Britain's largest thrush. It is also known as the 'stormcock', because it sings in the treetops when the wind is blowing hard. It forages on the ground for insects, worms and snails in spring and summer, and moves by bounding along in leaps. In winter, mistle thrushes feed on fruit and berries, especially yew, hawthorn, holly, mistletoe and ivy.

FACT FILE

Scientific name *Turdus viscivorus*

Size 26–28 cm

Wingspan 42–48 cm

Call Loud, rattling chatter 'tsarrk' or flute-like song

Breeding 3–5 eggs in two broods a year, from March to June

Mistle thrushes are usually shy of people, but they have been known to attack other animals, even dogs, during their breeding season.

Dark eye

Strong bill

Grey-brown back

Whitish breast with dark spots

Long wings

Powerful, long legs

REDWING

Redwings are most commonly seen in woods and fields, often in large flocks. They forage for worms, slugs, snails, insects and berries, sometimes in the company of fieldfares and song thrushes. Large groups may settle on one tree and stay there until they have stripped it of its berries. These birds are winter visitors to Britain, many of them travelling here from Scandinavia. They return to the continent in March, ready for the breeding season.

FACT FILE

Scientific name *Turdus iliacus*

Size 20–22 cm

Wingspan 33–35 cm

Call Variable songs from 'seep' to 'chuk'

Breeding 4–6 eggs, two broods, from April to July

Redwings travel far and wide to search for food, but they are very vulnerable to cold and a shortage of food. If there are no berries, they may die in their hundreds.

Bold white eye-stripe

Silver-white feathers on underside with speckles

Chestnut-red flanks

FIELDFARE

One of the largest types of thrush, fieldfares are social birds. They are often seen hopping along the ground. They visit gardens when they cannot find food in open fields and hedgerows. During autumn and winter, they can occasionally be seen eating ripe fruit that has fallen from trees. Fieldfares usually feed, fly and roost together in flocks.

Fieldfares migrate to the UK in winter, but they spend the rest of the year in Scandinavia where they breed. Nowadays, fewer fieldfares are seen in the UK.

Blue-grey head

Chestnut back

Short, thin, yellow beak

Speckled brown breast

Dark tail

BLACKBIRD

Male blackbirds are unmistakable visitors to the garden. They have all-black plumage, distinctive yellow bills and yellow rings around their eyes. Females are harder to spot as they are dull brown all over, except for a paler streak on their throats. Blackbirds can often be seen hopping along the ground, looking for food. When alarmed, they have a loud, shrill call that sounds like a 'chack-ak-chack-ak'.

FACT FILE

Scientific name *Turdus merula*
Size 23–30 cm
Wingspan 35–38 cm
Call Flute-like and loud
Breeding 4–5 light blue eggs with red spots, from March to April

Blackbirds often build their nests in open, exposed places where birds of prey and cats may reach them.

Yellow eye-ring

Yellow beak

Pure black plumage

SPOTTED FLYCATCHER

Slim birds, spotted flycatchers have grey-brown backs and pale undersides. Their eyes, beaks and legs are black. When they perch, spotted flycatchers flick their wings and tail. They can be found in habitats where there are trees, including gardens, parks and woodlands. These fast-flying birds catch their prey while on the wing. Damselflies and butterflies are two of their favourite prey.

FACT FILE

Scientific name
Muscicapa striata
Size 13–15 cm
Wingspan 23–25 cm
Call Soft but scratchy song
Breeding 4–5 pale blue eggs,
from May to June

The number of spotted flycatchers has dropped dramatically in recent years and they are now a threatened species. This may be due to loss of habitat.

Unusual streaked forehead

Long body

Speckled breast

Upright posture

GARDEN WARBLER

Despite their name, garden warblers prefer woodland to gardens, although they do visit gardens with mature trees. These birds are migrants and only come to the UK in summer, arriving in April and leaving in the middle of July. Their plain appearance helps to camouflage them, and they spend a lot of time in bushes and hedgerows, searching for insects and berries to eat.

FACT FILE

Scientific name *Sylvia borin*

Size 14 cm

Wingspan 20–22 cm

Call Melodic song

Breeding 3–7 dull cream eggs with grey spots, from late May to June

There are about 400 different types of warbler and many are dull in appearance. They are well-known for their melodious singing.

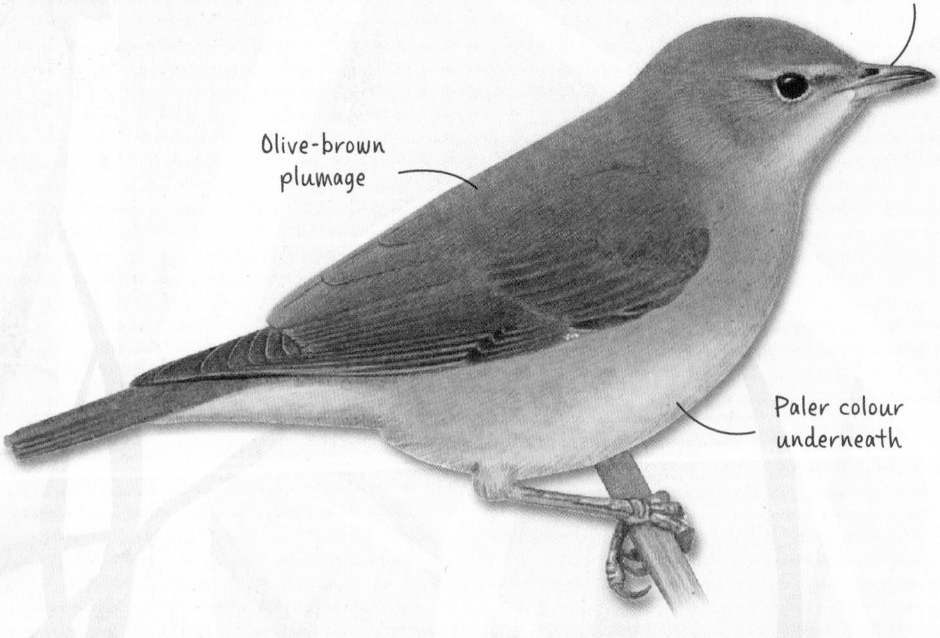

Small, slender beak
Olive-brown plumage
Paler colour underneath

BLACKCAP

In spring, the blackcap can be seen and heard singing from a high perch, often an oak tree. They work their way through brambles and undergrowth with garden warblers. Although mainly insect eaters, blackcaps eat berries and fruits in autumn. Increasing numbers of blackcaps are overwintering in Britain, and visiting bird tables during winter.

FACT FILE

Scientific name *Sylvia atricapilla*

Size 13–15 cm

Wingspan 20–23 cm

Call 'Tak' when disturbed, song is loud and warbling

Breeding 4–5 eggs, two broods, April to July

Blackcaps can be quite aggressive when competing for scraps in the garden, often frightening off much larger birds.

Males have a black cap

Grey-brown upperparts

Notched tail

WILLOW WARBLER

Flying in from North Africa every spring, the willow warbler is one of the most commonly seen summer visitors to Europe. On its arrival in Britain, it often feeds on insects found on flowering willows. These birds are always on the move, flicking their wings as they busily forage for insects. Willow warblers sing their songs from trees and bushes, while working their way through foliage seeking insects and while flying.

FACT FILE

Scientific name
Phylloscopus trochilus
Size 11 cm
Wingspan 17–22 cm
Call 'Hoo-id', song is a falling sequence of clear notes
Breeding 6–7 eggs, one brood, from April to May

When courting the female, the male willow warbler perches near her and slowly waves one or both of his wings at her.

Yellow eye-stripe

Olive-brown plumage

Pale, yellowish white underparts

Pale legs

CHIFFCHAFF

Chiffchaffs visit Britain in summer. However, in southern England and Ireland, some of them have given up migrating in winter and manage to survive the coldest months. These little birds are hard to spot because their olive-brown plumage hides them well in the vegetation. They are likely to be found close to water. Chiffchaffs eat insects and spiders that they find among leaves and flowers.

Young chiffchaffs stay in the nest for about two weeks before they are ready to fly. If any animal approaches them in the meantime, they will try to attack it.

Pale stripe over eye

Olive-brown plumage on back and head

Thin, short bill

Short wingtips

Grey-white underparts

Thin, dark legs

GOLDCREST

Europe's smallest bird, the goldcrest still manages to migrate across the North Sea from Scandinavia to spend the winter in Britain. The male goldcrest raises his bright crest when courting, and also when rivals stray into his territory. Their main food consists of spiders and small insects, such as aphids. Goldcrests are found in woodland, and in parks and gardens containing conifers, such as larch and fir.

FACT FILE

Scientific name *Regulus regulus*

Size 9 cm

Wingspan 13–16 cm

Call High-pitched 'zeek' and trill, also 'si-si-si'

Breeding 7–8 eggs, two broods, April to July

Goldcrests mingle with tits and firecrests, which are closely related, in food–hunting winter flocks.

Greenish back

Male has distinctive golden-orange crest, with a black stripe on each side

Fine moustache streak

Round body

LONG-TAILED TIT

Apart from its long tail, this is a tiny bird. They usually move in small flocks, seeking insects for food, and woods and hedgerows are good places to see them. These birds use their tiny beaks to harvest insects. They also feed on buds and small amounts of lichen and algae in the trees. Long-tailed tits were almost killed off by severe frosts in 1947 in Britain.

FACT FILE

Scientific name
Aegithalos caudatus

Size 14 cm

Wingspan 16–19 cm

Call 'Zee–zee' and 'trrr'

Breeding 8–12 eggs, one brood, from April to June

Because of their small size, long-tailed tits are vulnerable to cold, and flock members huddle together for warmth at night.

Bold eyebrow markings

Pink shoulder patches

Small, round body

Long tail

Fluffy pink-and-white plumage

BLUE TIT

Blue tits are small, lively birds and agile movers. They can hang upside down from twigs and bird feeders while eating, and can even perch on milk bottles to peck at the top and drink the milk. Blue tits have bright blue crowns and a yellow breast, with a slight black stripe. Females lay large clutches of eggs, and have been known to lay as many as 19 eggs in a single clutch.

FACT FILE

Scientific name
Cyanistes caeruleus

Size 11–12 cm

Wingspan 17–20 cm

Call Clear and high-pitched

Breeding 7–12 white eggs with purplish spots, from April to May

Blue tits are popular because they feed on aphids. These are small insects that damage plants. They also eat other insects including caterpillars, and nuts from feeders.

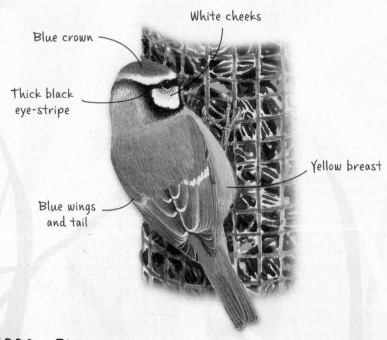

Blue crown

White cheeks

Thick black eye-stripe

Blue wings and tail

Yellow breast

GREAT TIT

The energetic and sprightly great tit is a common sight on a bird table, where it fights off other birds to get a bigger portion of food. It is the largest of all British tits, but is still very agile and acrobatic in its flying and perching skills, and can even swing upside down. Great tits have powerful bills that can be used to break tough nuts, but they can eat a wide variety of food, including insects, berries, nuts and seeds.

FACT FILE

Scientific name *Parus major*

Size 14 cm

Wingspan 22–25 cm

Call Very varied, e.g. 'chink', 'seetoo', 'tui-tui'

Breeding Five or more eggs, from April

Great tits originally lived in woodlands, but they have been drawn to gardens and parks by the food available in these new habitats.

Pale blue wings

Black crown

Blue-grey tail with white sides

White cheeks

Green back and bright yellow chest

COAL TIT

The smallest member of the tit family, coal tits are far more timid than blue tits. These birds will visit bird tables, but they carry food away and hide it. Coal tits are naturally birds of the forest. They forage in trees for live prey, such as spiders and insects, and search the ground for nuts and seeds. Acrobatic birds, coal tits can be seen creeping up tree trunks. They have a preference for deep woods of conifers.

FACT FILE

Scientific name *Parus ater*

Size 11.5 cm

Wingspan 17–21 cm

Call 'Tsui' or 'tsee'

Breeding Up to 11 eggs, one brood, April to June

Coal tits sometimes forage with mixed flocks of goldcrests and treecreepers through trees and bracken.

Black bib

White cheek and nape

White wing-bars

Small in size

MARSH TIT

The marsh tit is found in woodlands, where it hunts through the trees for insects and forages on the ground for seeds. It holds tough seeds, such as beechmast, with one foot while pecking them open with its strong beak. These birds often team up with flocks of several tit species. They appear in gardens in winter if food is put out.

FACT FILE

Scientific name *Poecile palustris*

Size 11.5 cm

Wingspan 18–19 cm

Call Shrill 'pitchu', song is 'chip, chip, chip'

Breeding 6–8 eggs, one brood, April to June

Marsh tits do not linger at the bird table. They carry food away to eat later, and hide it in the ground or in cracks in tree bark.

Small, black bib

Short bill

Glossy black cap

TREECREEPER

The treecreeper is an inconspicuous little bird, but is easily recognized by its long, curving beak, which it uses to probe bark as it creeps up tree trunks. Almost always working upwards from the bottom of the trunk, the treecreeper uses its stiff tail feathers as a support against the bark. As it moves upwards, it spirals around the tree trunk, then flies down to the bottom of the next tree.

FACT FILE

Scientific name
Certhia familiaris

Size 12.5 cm

Wingspan 18–21 cm

Call High-pitched 'tsit' or 'tsee'

Breeding 5–6 eggs, one brood, April to June

The treecreeper occasionally comes into gardens, but will not usually approach the bird table. It can be fed in the garden by smearing fat onto a tree trunk.

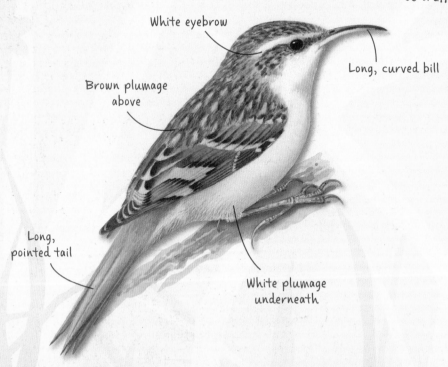

White eyebrow

Brown plumage above

Long, curved bill

Long, pointed tail

White plumage underneath

NUTHATCH

Unusual looking birds, nuthatches are often seen running up and down the trunks of trees, searching for insects. They use their sharp, pointed beaks to search cracks in tree bark for bugs or seeds. Males and females look similar, but the colours are slightly darker in males. They live in woodlands, but often visit gardens in search of nuts and seeds.

FACT FILE

Scientific name *Sitta europaea*

Size 11–15 cm

Wingspan 20–25 cm

Call Loud piping notes

Breeding 6–9 white eggs, from April to May

Nuthatches are easily mistaken for woodpeckers, as they both perch on the bark of trees. However nuthatches are the only birds that run headfirst down a tree.

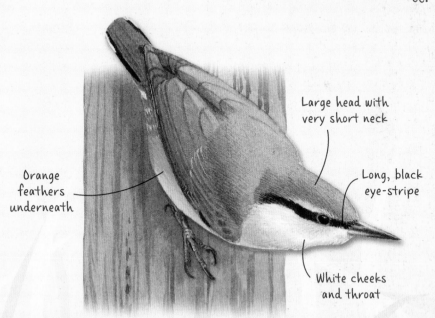

Large head with very short neck

Long, black eye-stripe

Orange feathers underneath

White cheeks and throat

MAGPIE

Large black-and-white birds, magpies have very long tails. Their tails are longer than their bodies and tinged with green. Magpies are most common in rural areas, especially near farms, but they often visit gardens and parks where they feed on rubbish and scraps. In spring, magpies can come together in large flocks called 'parliaments'. They are blamed for eating the eggs and nestlings of songbirds.

Magpies are believed to bring bad luck. However saying 'Good morning Mr Magpie' when you see one is supposed to ward off evil.

Dark-coloured head

Blue-black wings

Long, greenish-black tail with rounded tip

White feathers underneath

JAY

These birds are members of the crow family but, unlike most of their relatives, they have colourful plumage. Their bodies are pinky-brown and there are distinctive blue flashes on the wings. Jays are sociable birds, and males and females often stay together for life. They can copy the calls of other birds, but often make a loud screeching noise when they arrive in a garden.

FACT FILE

Scientific name
Garrulus glandarius
Size 31–35 cm
Wingspan 54–59 cm
Call Loud and harsh screech
Breeding 3–10 pale green, speckled eggs, from April to July

Jays feed on acorns and bury up to 3000 in one month. They sometimes forget about them, so the acorns grow into trees.

Streaked crown

Pinkish-brown body

White flash on the rump

Black moustache

Blue feathers on wing

Pink legs

CHOUGH

The chough is the rarest member of the crow family in Britain, and is easily distinguished from other crows. It is found along coastal cliffs, swooping along and calling loudly, and often flies in small flocks. The chough feeds inland of the cliffs on the fields where it nests. It eats insects and worms, as well as dropping down to sea level to eat little crabs and shellfish. It sometimes feeds on grain left in stubble after harvesting.

FACT FILE

Scientific name
Pyrrhocorax pyrrhocoraxs

Size 40 cm

Wingspan 73–90 cm

Call 'Kweeow' or 'chee-ah'.

Breeding 3–5 eggs

In 2002, wild chicks hatched in Cornwall, where the chough is the county's official bird, for the first time in 50 years.

Square-shaped tail

Curved red bill

All black feathers

JACKDAW

Small members of the crow family, jackdaws can survive in many different types of habitat and eat a wide variety of food. They usually live and roost in large groups, or colonies. They make their nests in a variety of places including rock faces, chimneys, churches and natural holes in trees. Jackdaws prey on the eggs and fledglings of woodpigeons and other birds. They also eat insects, worms and will forage on rubbish dumps.

FACT FILE

Scientific name
Corvus monedula

Size 33 cm

Wingspan 65–75 cm

Call Harsh calls, 'tchak'

Breeding 4–6 pale blue eggs, in April

Rooks, carrion crows and jackdaws can easily be mistaken for one another. However, these birds are quicker and more agile than most members of the crow family.

Paler feathers on neck

White eye-ring

Black, glossy plumage

CARRION CROW

Both male and female carrion crows have black plumage with stout, black bills. A close look at their feathers reveals a blue and purple shine. These crows live in a wide range of habitats, from gardens to coasts and mountains. Males and females share the job of building a nest, which is usually sited near the top of a tree, an electricity pylon or on a cliff edge.

FACT FILE

Scientific name *Corvus corone*

Size 44–50 cm

Wingspan 80–100 cm

Call Loud 'kraa-kraa'

Breeding 4–6 blotchy blue-green eggs, from April to May

Animals that feed on dead bodies are called carrion eaters. Although these crows eat carrion, they also feed on eggs, insects and grain.

All over black plumage with blue sheen

Short, heavy bill with small feathers at the base

Strong, perching toes with sharp claws

ROOK

The rook is one of the best-known British social birds, and lives in large flocks or colonies. Rooks often build their nests close to one another. In winter, the tops of trees may be home to many of these birds and their large nests. Rooks fly with a slow, flapping and gliding flight pattern. They feed on snails, larvae and grain, but may gather near roadsides to feed on animals that have been killed by vehicles.

FACT FILE

Scientific name
Corvus frugilegus

Size 44–46 cm

Wingspan 81–99 cm

Call Very loud raucous 'caaar'

Breeding 3–6 eggs, from March to June

There are more than one million breeding pairs of rooks in Britain. However, numbers dropped drastically in the 1960s because of pesticide poisoning.

Bare face

Black, glossy plumage

Long, thin, grey bill

Ragged-looking leg feathers and breast

Crows • BIRDS 187

STARLING

These birds have a reputation as one of the noisiest visitors to the garden. This is partly because they prefer to live and feed in large groups. These flocks are an amazing sight as they swoop into parkland or circle above a garden looking for suitable perches. Starlings are medium-sized birds that hold their bodies upright, as they busily march around looking for food. Their diet includes insects, worms, seeds and scraps.

FACT FILE

Scientific name
Sturnus vulgaris
Size 19–22 cm
Wingspan 37–43 cm
Call Twitters, clicks and whistles
Breeding 5–7 pale blue eggs, from April to May

Starlings are mimics — they can learn the songs of other birds and copy them. They don't stop at birdsong — they can also imitate car alarms and ring tones.

Small, light-coloured flecks on body and wings

Slender, yellow beak

Pointed wings

Metallic green-and-purple sheen on feathers

Short tail

HOUSE SPARROW

Small, active birds, sparrows are a familiar sight in the garden. Males have grey caps and chests, and a bold black patch on the throat and upper chest. They also have a black eye-stripe. Females are much duller in colour with a chestnut-coloured stripe over their eyes. Sparrows' nests are made from straw and grasses, and are lined with feathers.

FACT FILE

Scientific name
Passer domesticus
Size 14–15 cm
Wingspan 20–25 cm
Call Chirps
Breeding 3–5 pale blue eggs with grey blotches, from April to June

The house sparrow is becoming increasingly rare and has disappeared from some parts of the UK. No one knows for sure why their numbers are falling.

Grey cap

Yellow-brown beak in winter (black in summer)

Chestnut-brown plumage on back is darkly streaked

Black throat patch and eye-stripe

Grey breast

Pale brown legs

CHAFFINCH

Male chaffinches have rosy pink breasts and cheeks with bluish-grey heads. Females have greenish-brown backs and greyish-brown feathers underneath. Chaffinches have melodic songs, which differ from one region to another. They eat fruit, insects and seeds that they find on the ground, but they also catch insects in flight.

FACT FILE

Scientific name *Fringilla coelebs*
Size 14–16 cm
Wingspan 24–28 cm
Call Loud trills and short 'pink'
Breeding 2–8 light blue eggs, in April, incubated for 11–13 days

Chaffinches build their cup-shaped nests with grasses, mosses and lichens in the fork of a tree. The nests are lined with feathers and joined with spiders' webs.

Grey feathers on head

Bands of white on wings

Pink chest feathers

Brown tail

BRAMBLING

The brambling is very fond of beech woods, foraging through them in flocks sometimes numbering thousands. When beechmast crops fail or when the weather is particularly harsh, bramblings are attracted to gardens where food has been put out. These birds often move in mixed flocks containing chaffinches and other finches, as they hunt for insects and seeds on the woodland floor.

Bramblings are ground feeders, and they usually take the seeds and other scraps dropped from the bird table by other birds.

Black head and back with scaling in winter

White rump

Bright orange plumage

White belly

BULLFINCH

Bullfinches are often seen in couples, and are thought to pair for life. They are shy, and secretive birds, and like to stay close to cover. The bullfinch rarely forages on the ground, and is usually spotted in trees and bushes, using its strong beak to harvest seeds, berries and buds. In autumn and early winter, these birds feed on seeds, such as ash keys.

FACT FILE

Scientific name
Pyrrhula pyrrhula

Size 15 cm

Wingspan 22–26 cm

Call Distinct, low, piping 'phew'

Breeding 4–5 eggs, two broods,
April to June

Bullfinches are rare at the bird table, but they will take shelled peanuts from a net.

Black cap

Stubby, black bill

White rump

Rosy red breast

GOLDFINCH

Distinctive visitors to the garden, goldfinches are easy to identify. Males and females look alike – they have red faces with white cheeks and throats. The top of the head is black, and the wings have broad yellow bands. In winter, many goldfinches migrate south to warmer weather, returning in March and April, but some stay in the UK all year round.

FACT FILE

Scientific name
Carduelis carduelis
Size 12 cm
Wingspan 21–25 cm
Call Soft twills and twitters
Breeding 4–7 speckled blue eggs,
from May to August

It was once fashionable to have caged birds in the home, and goldfinches were a favourite because of their melodious song.

Brown back

Pinkish beak

Red, black and white face

White feathers underneath

Golden bars on black-and-brown wings

GREENFINCH

Greenfinches are stout birds that often live in groups, in hedges and other dense vegetation. Their bodies are mostly green, with yellow bands on their wings. Females and males look similar, but the females have more brown in their plumage. Greenfinches often come together in groups, or colonies, at breeding time. When the juveniles have left the nest, greenfinches may travel south for winter.

FACT FILE

Scientific name *Carduelis chloris*

Size 15 cm

Wingspan 25–28 cm

Call Wheezy song with whistles and twitters

Breeding 4–6 speckled cream eggs, from April to May

These birds are common in gardens, where they can find food easily. They like peanuts and sunflower seeds in particular.

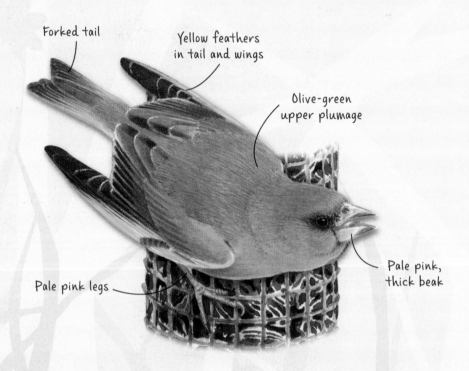

Forked tail

Yellow feathers in tail and wings

Olive-green upper plumage

Pale pink, thick beak

Pale pink legs

SISKIN

Siskins are commonly found in conifer woods. Their numbers have grown in recent years because of the increase of conifer plantations around Britain. They have spread further south and can now be found all across the country throughout the year. During winter, siskins often gather in large flocks, sometimes in the company of redpolls, which are a type of small finch.

Siskins love seeds, but they will visit gardens where they can find regular supplies of shelled peanuts. They also love the seeds of alder and birch trees.

Black crown

Bright yellow wing-bars

Black chin

Green-yellow breast

Grey-white belly and streaked flanks

YELLOWHAMMER

Small flocks of yellowhammers used to be a common sight on hedgerows, feeding on seeds or perched on telegraph wires singing all day long. Sadly, their numbers have declined drastically in recent years, putting the British population of these pretty songbirds at risk. The most likely reason for this is the loss of habitat, which has reduced their food supply. These birds are native and live in all regions of Britain.

FACT FILE

Scientific name
Emberiza citrinella
Size 15–17 cm
Wingspan 23–29 cm
Call Quick 'tsik' or trilling 'ti-ti-ti'
Breeding 3–5 eggs, up to three broods every year

The yellowhammer's song is sometimes described as sounding like 'a little bit of bread and no cheese'. With a little imagination, it is a good description!

Streaks on back

Mustard yellow head with dark stripes

Rust-coloured rump

Yellow belly and breast

Black tail

REED BUNTING

The reed bunting is a bird of the wetlands. However, it has now spread into some drier habitats. In winter, it leaves its reed beds and marshes, and moves to the fields. Here it hunts for seeds and insects alongside finches and other buntings. If threatened by approaching danger, the reed bunting pretends to be injured, crawling along with wings half spread, leading the threat away from its nest.

FACT FILE

Scientific name
Emberiza schoeniclus
Size 15.5 cm
Wingspan 21–26 cm
Call Loud 'tseek' and metallic 'chink'
Breeding 4–5 eggs, two broods, April to June

Reed buntings are primarily ground feeders, so are in danger of starvation when there is a covering of snow. They increasingly visit gardens in winter for food.

Black head

White collar

White moustache

White breast

COMMON FROG

Found in moist, shady habitats, common frogs often live in ponds, lakes or rivers. Adult frogs come together in spring to lay their eggs in water. One female can lay up to 2000 eggs, called spawn, in a clump. Young, or juvenile, frogs are called tadpoles. They live in water until they change into adults. They can survive cold winter months by sleeping in mud at the bottom of a pond.

FACT FILE

Scientific name
Rana temporaria
Size 6–8 cm
Habitat Shady, damp places
Hibernation November to February
Breeding Mating in spring, eggs laid in still water

Frogs have long, sticky tongues that they shoot out to catch flies and other insects. Frogs are friends to gardeners as they also eat pests, such as snails and slugs.

Rounded snout

Large eyes flecked with gold and brown

Fore limbs are shorter than hind limbs

Hind limbs have webbed toes

Skin is moist and is mottled brown and green in colour

COMMON TOAD

Common toads are found all over Britain, except northern Scotland, in damp or wet places. These amphibians are mostly nocturnal and eat a range of prey including spiders, worms, snails and slugs. Adults travel to pools and ponds in autumn, and as the cold weather draws in, they hibernate in leaf piles or burrows. In spring they mate, and males gather around the females in large groups. The females lay their eggs in water, which develop into tadpoles.

FACT FILE

Scientific name *Bufo bufo*
Size 5–9 cm
Habitat Watery or wet gardens, woods
Hibernation Late autumn to early spring
Breeding From March to June, 1000–3000 eggs are laid

Common toads produce a toxin from their skin. This prevents most predators from wanting to eat them.

Warty skin that produces toxins (poisons)

Brown, green or grey back and sides

Copper-coloured eye with horizontal pupil

White or grey underside

GREAT CRESTED NEWT

Easily recognized by their colourful bodies, which are covered in warty bumps, great crested newts are large amphibians. The upper body is usually muddy brown, grey or black, and the underside is bright orange or yellow, and covered in black marks. Males have a long crest on their back and a tail that grows bigger during the breeding season. These newts prefer moist habitats, such as ponds, to dry places, but they are able to travel a short distance from water.

FACT FILE

Scientific name
Triturus cristatus
Size 11–16 cm
Habitat Near pools and ponds
Hibernation October to February
Breeding Mating March to April, eggs laid in water

The tadpoles of the great crested newt look like adults, only smaller, when their legs have formed. They stay in water for four months before they can breathe air.

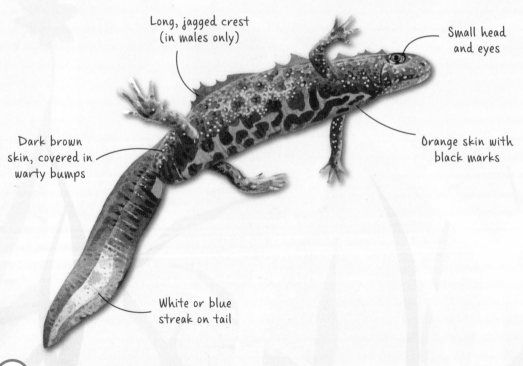

Long, jagged crest (in males only)

Small head and eyes

Dark brown skin, covered in warty bumps

Orange skin with black marks

White or blue streak on tail

Newts are amphibians – they spend part of their lives in water, and part on land. These newts live in damp places in summer and survive cold winter temperatures by hibernating. They have a similar diet to frogs and eat insects, caterpillars, slugs, tadpoles and snails, which they hunt near water. Juveniles (young) breathe in water using their gills, but adults breathe using their lungs and moist skin.

FACT FILE

Scientific name *Triturus vulgaris*

Size 7–11 cm

Habitat Damp places

Hibernation October to February

Breeding Mating in March and April, eggs laid in still water

Females lay up to 300 eggs at a time on water plant leaves. Each egg is wrapped individually by a leaf for protection.

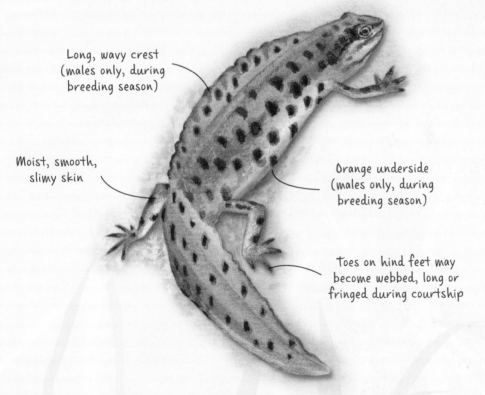

Long, wavy crest (males only, during breeding season)

Moist, smooth, slimy skin

Orange underside (males only, during breeding season)

Toes on hind feet may become webbed, long or fringed during courtship

ADDER

Adders are Britain's only venomous snakes. However, they are so secretive and non-aggressive that they do not pose any real danger to humans. These reptiles are found throughout Britain and are widespread in Scotland and parts of southern England. Adders are active in the day, and in warm weather they may be seen hunting for small animals, such as birds, lizards and frogs. They bite their prey with fangs, which inject venom, or poison, straight into the victim's flesh.

FACT FILE

Scientific name *Vipera berus*

Size 50–90 cm

Habitat Heaths, grassland, woods, moors

Hibernation September or October to March

Breeding 3–18 young born in August or September

Most reptiles lay eggs, but adders are viviparous snakes, which means they keep the eggs inside their bodies while they develop and give birth to live young.

Border of spots near zigzag

Vertical pupil

Dark zigzag pattern on the back

Males are grey, white or cream but females are red-brown

GRASS SNAKE

Shy animals, it is rare to see grass snakes even if they are present. Females are usually longer than males, and can reach up to 2 m in length. Grass snakes feed on a variety of animals, including mice, frogs, tadpoles, newts, fish and birds. They are excellent swimmers and spend much of their time in ponds and slow-moving waters.

FACT FILE

Scientific name *Natrix natrix*

Size 1.2–2 m

Habitat Low-growing vegetation

Hibernation October to March

Breeding Mating in March and April

If grass snakes are disturbed, they dive into water and hide among the weeds. They are excellent swimmers and can stay underwater for up to one hour.

Slender body

Greyish-green, scaly skin

Pale banding behind head

Dark marks along flanks of body

Pale underside

SLOW WORM

Despite their snake-like appearance, slow worms are actually limbless lizards. These reptiles are found throughout Britain, especially in southern regions and in gardens where they eat many pests. Their Latin name means 'fragile snake', which reflects the fact that they can easily drop off their tails if attacked. The tail continues to wriggle, distracting the predator while the lizard escapes. A new tail begins to grow in just two weeks.

FACT FILE

Scientific name *Anguis fragilis*

Size Up to 40 cm

Habitat Gardens, farms, parks, woods

Hibernation October to March

Breeding Mating occurs once in two years, eight live young are born August to September

Slow worms can live for many years – one individual lived to over 50.

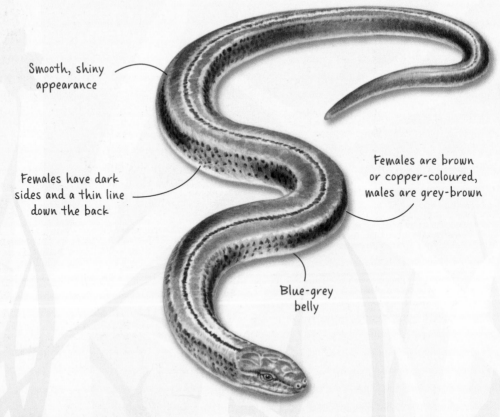

Smooth, shiny appearance

Females have dark sides and a thin line down the back

Females are brown or copper-coloured, males are grey-brown

Blue-grey belly

COMMON LIZARD

Lizards are reptiles and, unlike newts, can spend all their lives on land. Their skin is dry and scaly, and they often bask in the sun to warm their bodies. The viviparous lizard is also known as the common lizard. It has short legs and a very long tail, which may be twice the length of the body. The colours and patterns vary, but most are mixed shades of green and brown. Males are darker than females. These lizards are good swimmers.

FACT FILE

Scientific name
Lacerta vivipara
Size 10–15 cm
Habitat Open areas
Hibernation October to March
Breeding Mating in spring and young are born from June onwards

Most reptiles lay eggs. However, viviparous lizards keep their eggs inside their bodies until they are ready to hatch. Between three and 20 eggs hatch in a litter.

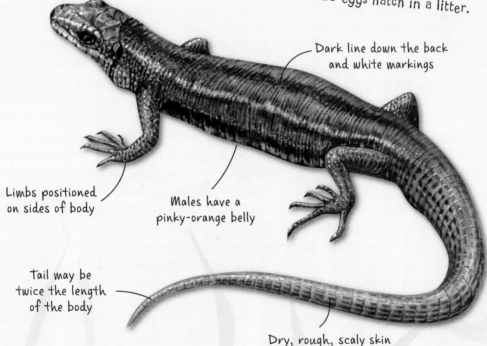

Dark line down the back and white markings

Limbs positioned on sides of body

Males have a pinky-orange belly

Tail may be twice the length of the body

Dry, rough, scaly skin

BROWN TROUT

It is difficult to identify brown trout because their appearance can vary enormously, depending on where they live. Some are dull with deep colours, while others are bright and speckled. They can also be difficult to spot because these large fish like to hide beneath cover, and are most likely to be found resting along riverbanks or under bridges. Trout are predators, and have rows of sharp teeth in their large mouths. They eat insects, worms and crustaceans.

FACT FILE

Scientific name *Salmo trutta*

Size Up to 30 cm

Habitat From small brooks to large rivers and lakes

Found Widespread

Breeding Spawning in winter, eggs hatch in 3–4 months

Like some other fish, trout eggs and young fish (larvae) can take a long time to mature into adults — up to four years. They develop more slowly in cold water.

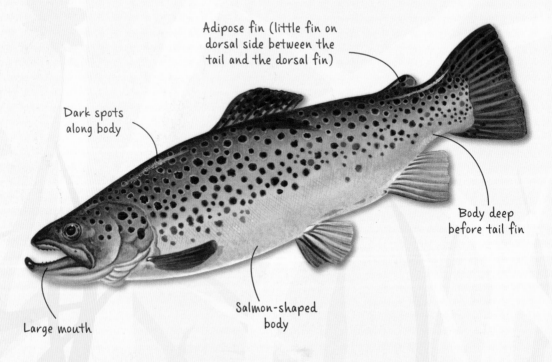

Adipose fin (little fin on dorsal side between the tail and the dorsal fin)

Dark spots along body

Body deep before tail fin

Large mouth

Salmon-shaped body

COMMON CARP

Carp were first introduced to Britain in the 1300s, possibly from the river Danube in Europe, where a wild population still exists. They have been bred for centuries and have often been kept in ponds as ornamental fish. Now they are found in many bodies of water and they are common throughout Britain. These freshwater fish eat plants and small animals that they find in the muddy sediment at the bottom.

FACT FILE

Scientific name *Cyprinus carpio*

Size Up to 1.2 m

Habitat Slow-moving or still fresh water

Found Widespread

Breeding Spawning in the summer, up to one million eggs

There are different types of common carp, including leather carp, with no scales, king carp and mirror carp, with a single row of shiny scales on the sides.

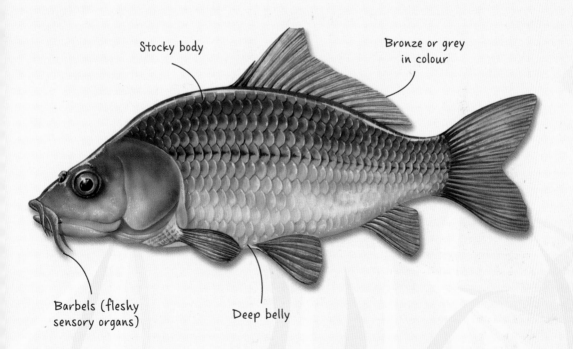

Stocky body

Bronze or grey in colour

Barbels (fleshy sensory organs)

Deep belly

MINNOW

Minnows live in large groups, or shoals, and are most commonly found in bodies of water that are clean and contain plenty of oxygen. They live throughout Britain, except northern Scotland. These small fish feed on plants, algae, insects, molluscs and crustaceans. In springtime, they swim to shallow, pebbled stretches of river where they mate and lay their eggs. At this time, males change appearance, becoming brighter and developing different colours to females.

FACT FILE

Scientific name
Phoxinus phoxinus
Size 6–10 cm
Habitat Clean streams or rivers
Found Widespread
Breeding Spawning from April–June, adults migrate upstream to spawning areas

Minnows are an important source of food for many other animals that share their habitat. Kingfishers, herons, otters and larger fish all prey upon them.

Large eyes

Blunt snout

Brown-green back

Darker spots create a band

Small mouth

Lower fins and belly will turn red in males at breeding time

ROACH

Common freshwater fish, roach are widespread throughout all of Europe. It is easiest to spot them in the spring, when they become very active around breeding time. They mostly eat insect larvae and small molluscs, but roach themselves are eaten by herons, pikes, eels, mink and some birds of prey. These fish are also caught by anglers in large numbers. Roach are slow-growing and do not reach maturity until two to three years of age.

FACT FILE

Scientific name *Rutilus rutilus*

Size 10–25 cm

Habitat Freshwater lakes, canals, slow-moving rivers

Found Widespread

Breeding Spawning from April–June, up to 100,000 eggs

Roach are able to live in dirty water, and water with some salt (which is described as 'brackish'). They are able to cope with most conditions and many habitats.

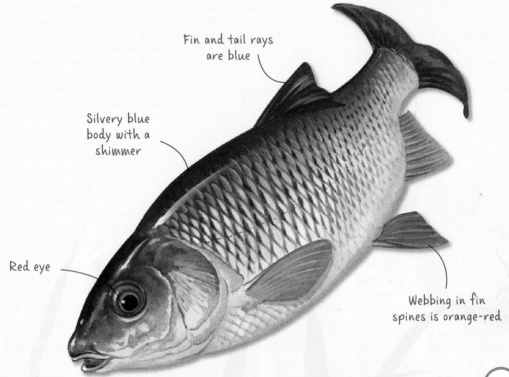

Fin and tail rays are blue

Silvery blue body with a shimmer

Red eye

Webbing in fin spines is orange-red

SALMON

These fish are among the most interesting of British wildlife. They lead extraordinary lives that involve impressive migrations to the open sea and back again. They also feature in a famous autumn spectacle when they leap upstream to their spawning grounds. When water levels are high, these large fish hurl themselves up rivers and over weirs and waterfalls, before mating. Adults spend most of their lives at sea, eating squid, shrimp and small fish and they only return to fresh water to breed.

FACT FILE

Scientific name *Salmo salar*

Size Up to 1.5 m

Habitat Open ocean, clean rivers

Found Scotland and some scattered rivers elsewhere

Breeding Spawning in November

Until the 19th century, people thought that young salmon were a completely different species from the adults, and no one understood their complicated life cycles.

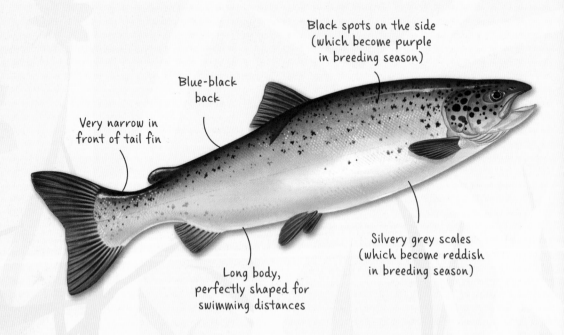

Black spots on the side (which become purple in breeding season)

Blue-black back

Very narrow in front of tail fin

Long body, perfectly shaped for swimming distances

Silvery grey scales (which become reddish in breeding season)

THREE-SPINED STICKLEBACK

These sticklebacks are common in coastal areas or in freshwater, where there is plenty of vegetation to protect them from predators. They prefer places that have muddy or sandy bottoms. These fish usually live in large groups and feed on crustaceans, worms, insects, small fish, eggs and young fish (fry) of other species. At breeding time, male sticklebacks become very aggressive and may attack anything that is red, which they mistake for other males.

FACT FILE

Scientific name *Gasterosteus aculeatus aculeatus*

Size 4–6 cm

Habitat Freshwater and seawater

Found Widespread

Breeding Spawning in spring and summer; eggs laid in nest

Male sticklebacks build a nest and once the female has laid the eggs, he takes care of them. He fans the eggs with his fins to keep oxygen passing over them.

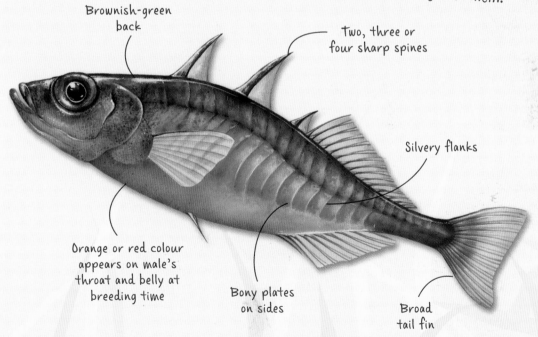

Brownish-green back

Two, three or four sharp spines

Silvery flanks

Orange or red colour appears on male's throat and belly at breeding time

Bony plates on sides

Broad tail fin

EARTHWORM

Earthworms are animals with soft bodies that are divided into many segments. They do not have legs and move by rhythmically contracting and relaxing their muscles. They also have little bristles, called setae, which help them to move through burrows of soil. Earthworms spend most of their time underground, where it is moist. They swallow soil and eat decaying plant matter. Earthworms are good for gardens as they improve soil by bringing air into it.

FACT FILE

Scientific name
Lumbricus terrestris

Habitat Underground, compost heaps

Breeding Young are small, but fully formed worms

Earthworms are unusual because they have both male and female reproductive organs. They do not fertilize themselves, however, and still come together to mate.

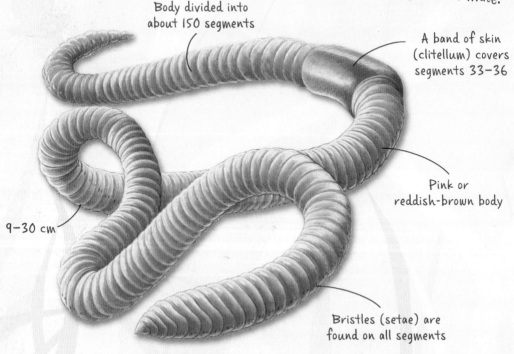

Body divided into about 150 segments

A band of skin (clitellum) covers segments 33–36

Pink or reddish-brown body

9–30 cm

Bristles (setae) are found on all segments

SLUG

Netted slugs are light brown or grey in colour and are one of the most frequent slug visitors to gardens. They are herbivorous and eat a wide range of plants, particularly those with tender, sweet leaves such as seedlings. The garden slug is bluish-black with a pale underside. It produces orangey-yellow slime and feeds on garden plants such as lettuces, seedlings and strawberries. They are unwelcome visitors to the garden because they destroy so many plants.

FACT FILE

Scientific name
Deroceras reticulatum

Habitat Damp places, such as soil and under plants

Breeding Young are small slugs

When disturbed, slugs produce a liquid, called slime. It is used for protection, and to create a smooth surface for movement. It is sticky and swells when it absorbs water.

Two pairs of feelers or tentacles

Area behind head is called the mantle

Grey or light brown body

40–55 mm

Netted pattern on body

BROWN-LIPPED SNAIL

Brown-lipped snails are very similar to white-lipped snails, both in appearance and lifestyle. Their name indicates the best way to identify them – brown-lipped snails have a dark band on the rim of the shell. These molluscs are most active at night, when the ground is damp. They feed on grass and other low-growing plants, and are regarded by gardeners as destructive pests. Brown-lipped snails are also known as grove snails and are very common throughout Britain.

FACT FILE

Scientific name
Cepaea nemoralis

Habitat Woods, hedges and gardens

Breeding Male and female parts, can fertilize own eggs

A cluster of empty snail shells next to a rock suggests that a thrush has been at work. These birds bash snails against a hard surface to break them.

Different banding patterns

Shell is brown, pale yellow or pinkish

Brown lip on margin of shell

Conical spire

Glossy, thin walls on shell

18–22 mm

GARDEN SNAIL

Most snails live in water, but land snails are often found in gardens. Garden snails are quite large and have a brown or yellowy-brown shell with dark markings. They feed on plants, usually at night, when the soil is damp. Garlic snails are only 6–10 mm long and have glossy, dark-brown shells. They live in leaf litter and compost heaps, and eat fungi or rotting plants.

FACT FILE

Scientific name *Helix aspersa*

Habitat Damp places, such as compost heaps

Breeding Young are small snails

Snails belong to the same family as octopuses and squid — molluscs. These animals have soft bodies and no skeleton, although some molluscs have protective shells.

Large, round shell patterned with brown and cream

Shell has up to five spirals

Two pairs of sensitive feelers, or tentacles

Soft body moves on a film of slime

25–40 mm

WOODLOUSE

Common creatures in a garden habitat, woodlice eat rotting material and use their senses of sight and smell to find food. Woodlice often eat in a group, under stones or vegetation, where they can hide from predators. When threatened, woodlice flatten their bodies and clamp themselves to a stone or wood. After mating, females carry their eggs in a special 'brood pouch' until they are ready to hatch.

FACT FILE

Scientific name
Oniscus asellus

Habitat Soil and compost heaps

Breeding Young are called stadia

Woodlice are not insects, but crustaceans, like shrimps and lobsters. Most crustaceans live in the oceans but woodlice can survive on land.

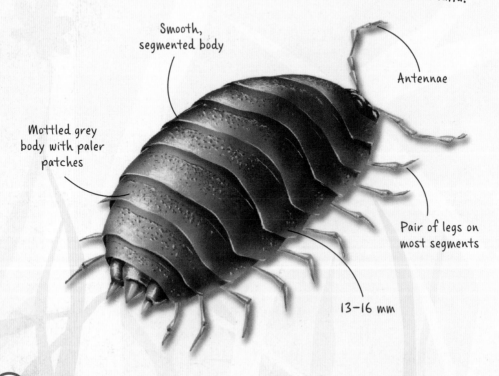

Smooth, segmented body

Antennae

Mottled grey body with paler patches

Pair of legs on most segments

13–16 mm

SILVERFISH

Silverfish are very common insects and it is easiest to see them at night, when they are most active. They prefer damp habitats, such as bathrooms. Silverfish scavenge whatever food they can find, but mostly eat starchy food, such as mould, paper, flour and glue. The nymphs that hatch from eggs moult many times before becoming adults.

FACT FILE

Scientific name
Lepisma saccharina
Habitat Houses and sheds
Breeding Small nymphs

These tough little insects have been known to survive for a whole year without food.

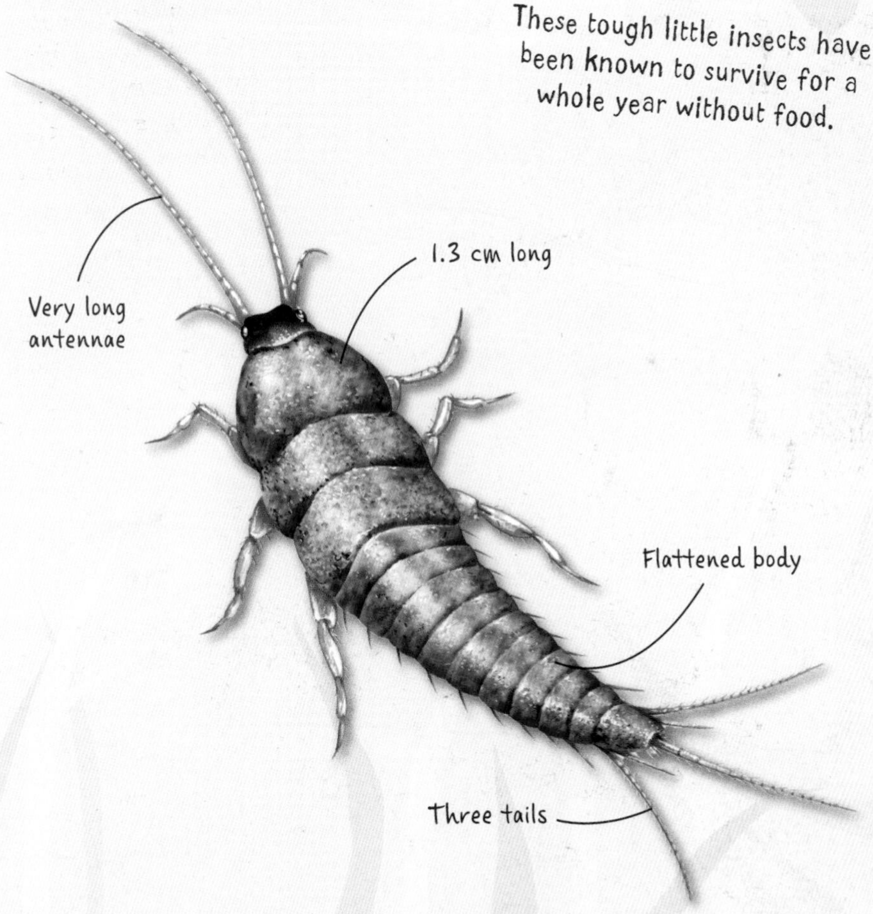

Very long antennae

1.3 cm long

Flattened body

Three tails

DRAGONFLY

Dragonflies are superb flyers. They dart around in summer and autumn, visiting woodlands and gardens where there is water. They can be easily recognized by their long, slender bodies with colourful bands. Dragonflies have huge eyes that almost meet, and give them great vision. These insects spend most of their early lives underwater in ponds or lakes as nymphs. They breathe using gills.

FACT FILE

Scientific name
Odonata order

Habitat Near slow-moving or still water

Breeding Young are called nymphs

In ancient times, dragonflies were much bigger than they are today. Fossils of dragonflies show that their wingspans reached up to 75 cm!

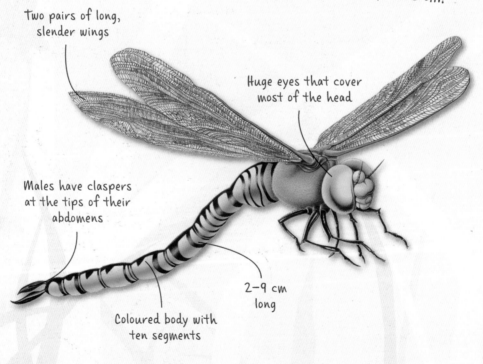

Two pairs of long, slender wings

Huge eyes that cover most of the head

Males have claspers at the tips of their abdomens

Coloured body with ten segments

2–9 cm long

SCORPIONFLY

Scorpionflies mostly feed on dead insects and they have tough, biting mouthparts that can tackle crunchy skins. They find their food in spiders' webs. Males have swollen tails that look like scorpion stingers. In fact, these organs are used during mating. Female scorpionflies sometimes like to eat their mates, so males present them with a gift of a drop of saliva before mating, to prevent an untimely death.

FACT FILE

Scientific name
Panorpa communis

Habitat Gardens, woodlands and hedgerows

Breeding Larvae resemble caterpillars

Both adults and larvae eat dead animals, especially insects.

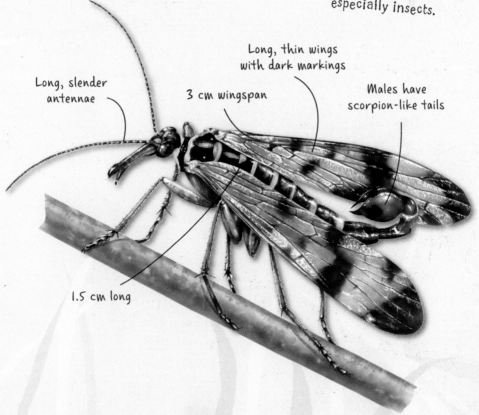

Long, slender antennae

3 cm wingspan

Long, thin wings with dark markings

Males have scorpion-like tails

1.5 cm long

GRASSHOPPER

With large wings, grasshoppers are good flyers, but they prefer to escape from danger by leaping. Usually green in colour, they are well camouflaged against foliage. They have long, powerful legs that they use for jumping more than 20 times their own body length. Crickets have longer antennae than grasshoppers and can often be heard 'singing' on a summer's evening. The song sounds like a series of loud 'chirrups'.

In some parts of the world, grasshoppers are a popular food. Their legs and wings are removed before the body is fried in oil.

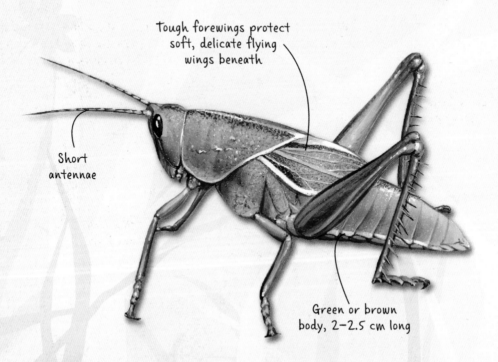

Tough forewings protect soft, delicate flying wings beneath

Short antennae

Green or brown body, 2–2.5 cm long

SPECKLED BUSH CRICKET

These insects are the smallest British crickets, but they are common. The adults feed on leaves through summer, especially on those of rose and raspberry bushes. Other crickets stop chirping in late summer, but speckled bush crickets make their soft noises well into autumn, although they can be hard to hear.

FACT FILE

Scientific name
Leptophyes punctatissima

Habitat Grasslands, gardens and parks

Breeding Eggs are laid in cracks in bark

Most crickets have two pairs of working wings, but a speckled bush cricket's wings are too small to be of any use.

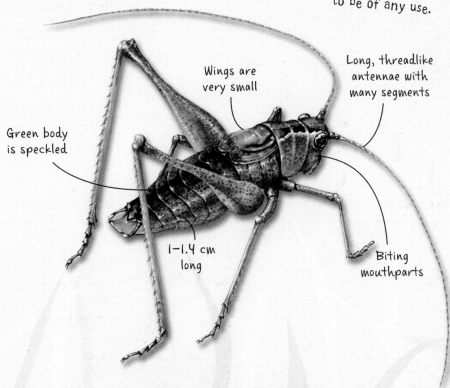

Wings are very small

Long, threadlike antennae with many segments

Green body is speckled

1–1.4 cm long

Biting mouthparts

LACEWING

Green lacewings have slender, delicate bodies and long, flimsy wings that are veined and almost transparent. There are more than 1600 species of lacewing and most of them are only active at night. They are predators and attack all sorts of other insects, especially those with soft bodies, such as caterpillars and aphids. They are often bred in large numbers and released on farmland to reduce the number of pests, without the need for chemical pesticides.

FACT FILE

Scientific name
Chrysopidae family

Habitat Woodland, farms and gardens

Breeding Eggs are laid on long stalks to protect them from ants and other predators

Lacewings are equipped with sensors on their wings. These can detect ultrasound, which is a type of noise produced by bats, so lacewings can avoid being eaten by them.

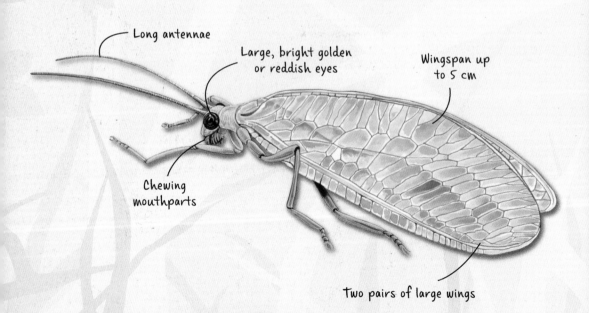

Long antennae

Large, bright golden or reddish eyes

Wingspan up to 5 cm

Chewing mouthparts

Two pairs of large wings

EARWIG

Plentiful in most gardens, earwigs are often found lurking in cracks and crevices where it is dark and they are hidden from predators. They have long, thin bodies and two pairs of wings – the first of which are leathery and short. Earwigs have pincers, called cerci, on the ends of their abdomen. Cerci are used to help fold the wings back after flight.

FACT FILE

Scientific name
Forficula auricularia

Habitat In soil and under stones

Breeding Young earwigs appear white when they moult

It was once believed that earwigs climbed into people's ears and burrowed into the brain. Mashed earwigs were used in Roman times to treat earache.

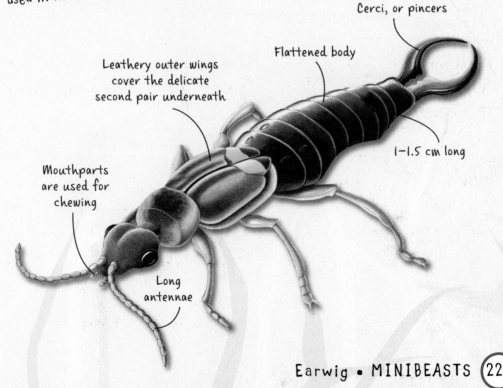

Cerci, or pincers

Flattened body

Leathery outer wings cover the delicate second pair underneath

1–1.5 cm long

Mouthparts are used for chewing

Long antennae

ANT

Found in almost every habitat on land in the world, ants live in large colonies. They can be seen busily scurrying around a garden from spring to autumn, but are seen less often in winter when the temperatures are low. A colony of ants is divided into different types – the queen ant, female workers and male ants. Some defend the nest, for example, while others are involved in reproduction.

FACT FILE

Scientific name
Formicidae family

Habitat Underground and compost heaps

Breeding Queens lay thousands of eggs every month

Colonies in tropical regions can contain millions of ants. Some, such as driver and army ants, eat almost anything and can strip a tethered horse to its skeleton.

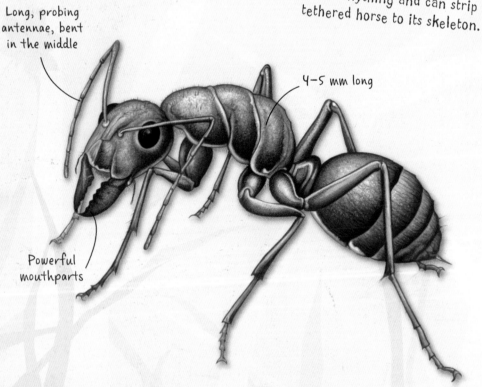

Long, probing antennae, bent in the middle

4–5 mm long

Powerful mouthparts

BEE

One of the most important groups of insect, bees benefit gardeners and farmers. They pollinate many plants, which is an essential part of fruit and seed production. Some bees, such as honeybees, collect nectar from plants and feed pollen to their young. They are not aggressive insects and rarely sting. However, unlike honeybees, bumblebees can sting more than once. Some types of bumblebee are in danger of becoming extinct.

FACT FILE

Scientific name *Apidae* family

Habitat Gardens, woodlands and parks

Breeding Queens lay more than 100 eggs a day

Bees communicate with each other in different ways, including 'dancing'. Honeybees returning to the hive use a dance to tell other bees where to find nectar.

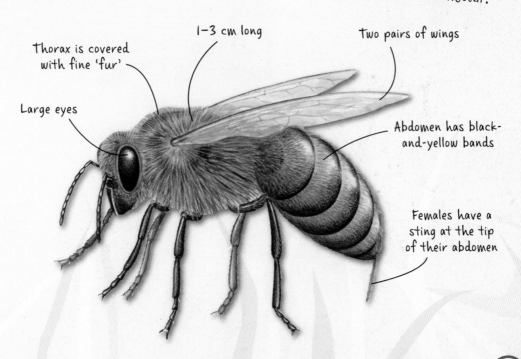

Thorax is covered with fine 'fur'

1–3 cm long

Two pairs of wings

Large eyes

Abdomen has black-and-yellow bands

Females have a sting at the tip of their abdomen

WASP

Common wasps live in large colonies, in a big nest made out of chewed wood fibres. They often choose to nest near or in houses and may become troublesome, because they can inflict painful stings. Queens are the only females that reproduce and they come out of hibernation in spring, ready to start a new colony. The first eggs she lays produce female workers, and later on her eggs produce males and new queens.

FACT FILE

Scientific name
Vespula vulgaris

Habitat Gardens and woodlands

Breeding Larvae grow in cells or 'combs'

Wasps belong to the same family of insects as bees and ants. Larvae feed on insects and adults feed on nectar or other sugary substances, such as rotting fruit.

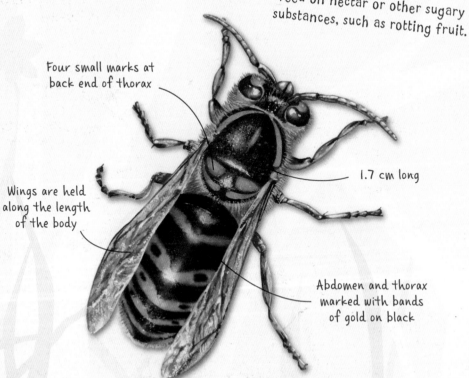

Four small marks at back end of thorax

1.7 cm long

Wings are held along the length of the body

Abdomen and thorax marked with bands of gold on black

HORNTAIL

These fierce looking insects are sometimes called wood wasps and, although they look like stinging wasps, they are harmless. The long spike from a female's abdomen may appear to be a sting, but is actually an ovipositor – an organ the female uses to lay her eggs into wood. The larvae have small legs and strong mouthparts. They live inside a tree and feed on its wood for up to two years before turning into pupae.

FACT FILE

Scientific name
Urocerus gigas

Habitat Conifer woodlands

Breeding Eggs are laid
in trunks

Female horntails are black and yellow. Males have an orange abdomen, with a black tip, and orange legs. They are smaller than females.

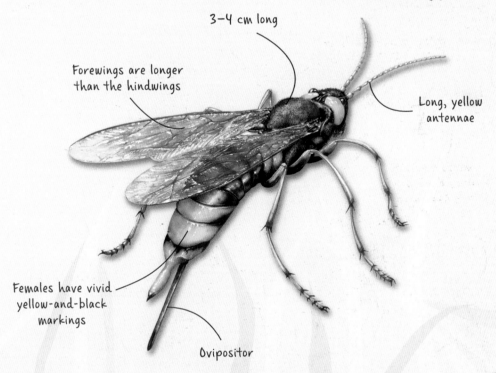

3–4 cm long

Forewings are longer than the hindwings

Long, yellow antennae

Females have vivid yellow-and-black markings

Ovipositor

HOVERFLY

Skilled flyers, hoverflies only have one pair of wings, and they dart about and change direction with speed. Adults are often seen near flowering plants, making a high-pitched buzzing sound as they forage for nectar and pollen. They can hover in one place, with their wings beating so fast that the movement cannot be seen by the human eye.

FACT FILE

Scientific name
Syrphus ribesii

Habitat Gardens, parks and woodlands

Breeding Green or yellow sluglike larvae

Hoverfly larvae emerge from small, white, oval eggs. They are blind and limbless, and have enormous appetites. Several generations hatch in one year.

One pair of wings (wasps have two pairs)

8–10 mm long

Black-and-yellow bands on abdomen

Large eyes made up of many small lenses

Mouthparts are used to feed on pollen and nectar

HORSE FLY

Horse flies are amongst the largest of all flies and there are more than 4000 species of them in the world. In Britain they are often found near wet habitats or around farms. Females bite humans or other animals and have razor-sharp mouthparts for cutting skin. They bite to get protein, which helps them produce bigger and healthier clusters of eggs. However, males suck nectar. The larvae are maggots, which live in mud and feed on rotting matter or small insects.

Females use their enormous eyes to help them find their prey to bite. They can also detect carbon dioxide, the gas that humans and other animals breathe out.

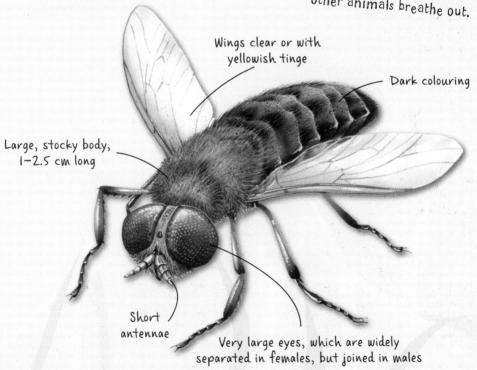

Wings clear or with yellowish tinge

Dark colouring

Large, stocky body, 1–2.5 cm long

Short antennae

Very large eyes, which are widely separated in females, but joined in males

BLUEBOTTLE

Easily recognized by the shiny metallic sheen to their body, bluebottles belong to a group of insects called blowflies. They visit gardens where there is rubbish, food or animal faeces, and they are unwelcome visitors since they spread diseases. When the eggs hatch, small, white carrot-shaped maggots emerge to feed and grow. The maggots dig into the ground and pupate, emerging as adult flies about ten days later.

FACT FILE

Scientific name
Calliphora vomitoria

Habitat Gardens and houses

Breeding Larvae are called maggots

Blowflies eat the flesh of living animals. They lay their eggs in open wounds, the maggots hatch within eight hours, and then eat the flesh.

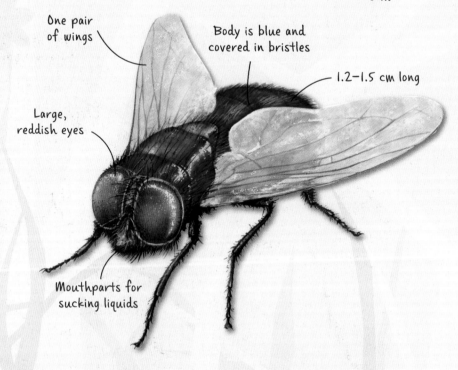

One pair of wings

Body is blue and covered in bristles

1.2–1.5 cm long

Large, reddish eyes

Mouthparts for sucking liquids

CRANE FLY

Crane flies are more commonly known as daddy-long-legs. They have long, slender bodies and unusually long legs. In tropical regions, their legs can measure up to 10 cm, but 3–6 cm is normal in cooler places. Adults are usually seen in gardens in autumn, especially during periods of damp or foggy weather. The larvae live in soil, where they feed on roots.

Crane flies are slow and easy to catch. They have small balancing limbs, called halteres, on either side of their bodies, which help to keep them stable when they fly.

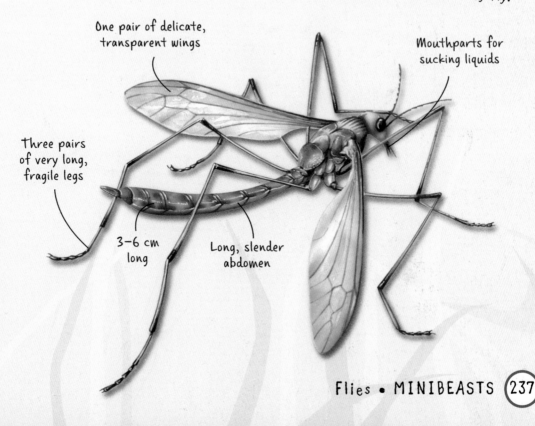

One pair of delicate, transparent wings

Mouthparts for sucking liquids

Three pairs of very long, fragile legs

3–6 cm long

Long, slender abdomen

GNAT

Gnats are very common insects and they make a familiar humming sound when they fly at night. The adults lay their eggs in layers, called rafts, on the surface of water. When the larvae hatch they hang from the surface, then sink to the bottom of the body of water when they turn into pupae. The adults are able to survive cold winters by hibernating.

Gnats sometimes bite humans, but they mostly bite birds, which in turn eat gnats.

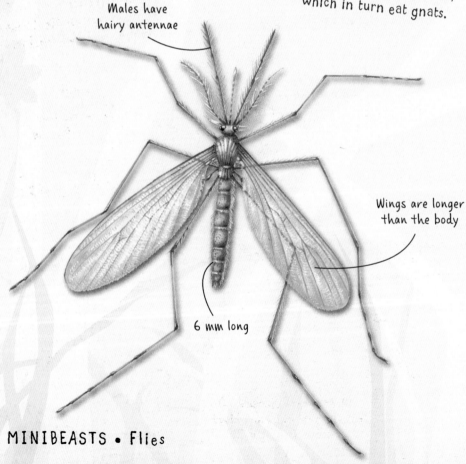

Males have hairy antennae

Wings are longer than the body

6 mm long

MOSQUITO

In spring, adult mosquitoes emerge from the water where they have lived as larvae. They can survive until winter and some adults hibernate. Males feed on nectar and other plant juices, but females need blood meals before they can lay their eggs. Mosquitoes have long mouthparts that they use to pierce skin (human or animal) and suck up blood. They are found near ponds, rivers and stagnant pools of water.

FACT FILE

Scientific name
Aedes detritus

Habitat Near slow-moving
or still water

Breeding Larvae live in water

In hot regions of the world, mosquitoes spread deadly diseases, such as malaria and dengue fever, to people. Only female Anopheles mosquitoes spread malaria.

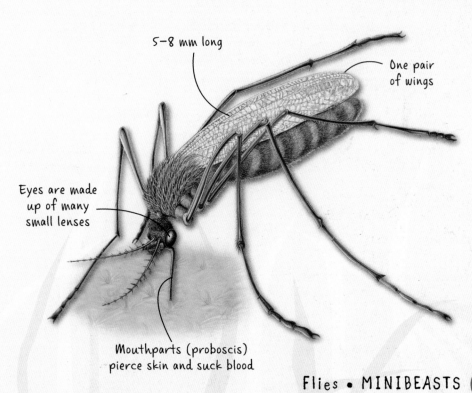

5-8 mm long

One pair
of wings

Eyes are made
up of many
small lenses

Mouthparts (proboscis)
pierce skin and suck blood

APHID

There are about **4000 types of aphid and many of those are garden pests.** The most well-known aphid is the common greenfly, which lives on plants. Aphids use their long, slender mouthparts to pierce a hole in the stems of plants. Then they eat the liquid food that pours out of the hole. Aphids also damage plants by passing viruses between them. Ladybirds and lacewings are predators of aphids.

FACT FILE

Scientific name
Aphidae family

Habitat Tender plant stems, leaves and buds

Breeding Seasonal

Aphids produce a sticky substance called honeydew, which ants collect for food. In return, the ants protect the aphids from other predators.

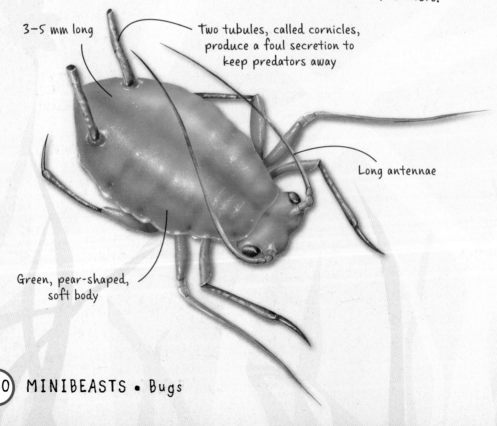

3–5 mm long

Two tubules, called cornicles, produce a foul secretion to keep predators away

Long antennae

Green, pear-shaped, soft body

WHITEFLY

There are many different types of whitefly that attack garden plants, house plants and greenhouse plants. They lay their eggs on the leaves of their host and both the larvae and adults feed on sap. This causes some damage but also passes viruses between plants. Tens of thousands of whitefly can live on a single tree or vegetable crop. Whiteflies have a very short life cycle and can go from egg to adult in just three weeks.

FACT FILE

Scientific name
Aleyrodes species

Habitat Farms and gardens

Breeding Larvae are called nymphs

Whiteflies are attracted to yellow, so gardeners sometimes plant marigolds near their crops to encourage the whitefly to feed on them instead.

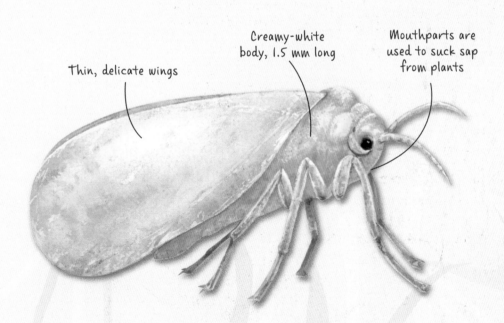

Thin, delicate wings

Creamy-white body, 1.5 mm long

Mouthparts are used to suck sap from plants

GREEN SHIELD BUG

Often found resting on leaves in the sun, green shield bugs are broad and flat in shape. They have hard forewings that protect the second pair of wings. Their sucking mouthparts are used to drink sap from plants. The larvae are similar in shape to adults, but they are black and green. Adults spend winter hibernating in leaf litter and in spring, females lay up to 400 eggs on plants.

Shield bugs may look like beetles, but actually they belong to a different group of insects called bugs, or hemipterans.

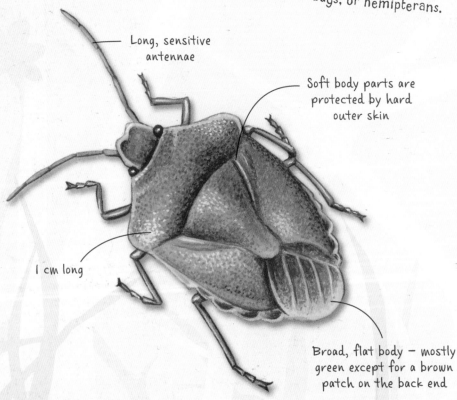

Long, sensitive antennae

Soft body parts are protected by hard outer skin

I cm long

Broad, flat body — mostly green except for a brown patch on the back end

GREEN CAPSID BUG

I**t may not be easy to see capsids, but the damage they do to fruit crops is often obvious.** When they feed on fruits, such as apples, pears and strawberries, capsids leave small brown spots, which lead to strange-looking fruits. The nymphs look like their parents and they feed on the new shoots growing on the plants.

FACT FILE

Scientific name
Lygocoris pabulinus
Habitat Anywhere there are plants
Breeding Lays eggs on plants

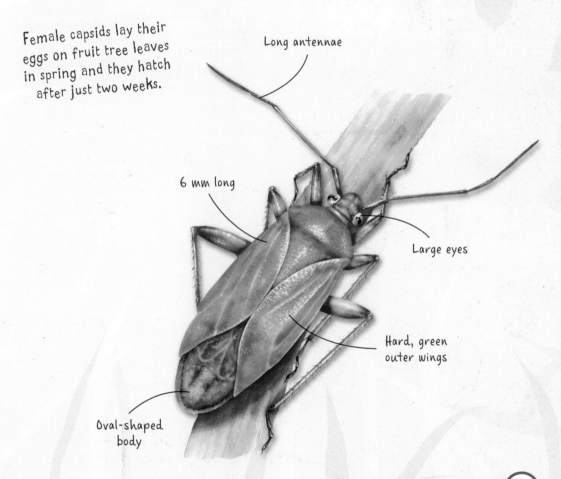

Female capsids lay their eggs on fruit tree leaves in spring and they hatch after just two weeks.

Long antennae

6 mm long

Large eyes

Hard, green outer wings

Oval-shaped body

LESSER WATER BOATMAN

These bugs swim in ponds and eat plant matter, often scraping algae off rocks or other surfaces. They use their unusually long legs like paddles as they move swiftly through the water. They are preyed upon by animals, such as dragonfly larvae and birds. Although lesser water boatmen look similar to water boatmen, or common backswimmers, they actually belong to a different group of bugs.

FACT FILE

Scientific name
Corixa punctata

Habitat Ponds and canals

Breeding Eggs are laid in spring and are attached to plants

Lesser water boatmen swim on their fronts, while water boatmen swim on their backs. They are predators, hunting tadpoles, small fish and flying insects that fall into the water.

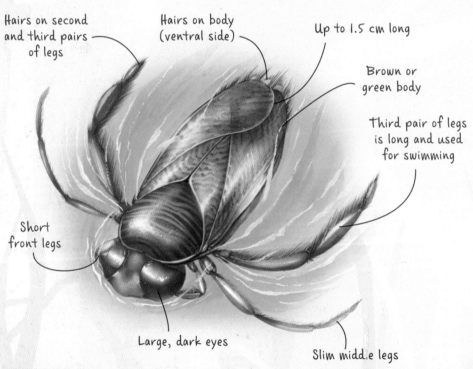

Hairs on second and third pairs of legs

Hairs on body (ventral side)

Up to 1.5 cm long

Brown or green body

Third pair of legs is long and used for swimming

Short front legs

Large, dark eyes

Slim midd.e legs

POND SKATER

Pond skaters are fascinating creatures to watch as they speed across water without breaking its surface. These bugs are also known as waterstriders and they are widespread throughout Britain. Pond skaters can detect prey by sensing vibrations on the water surface caused when an insect falls into the water. Within seconds, the pond skater can locate its prey and it then grabs it with its short, stout front legs. If attacked themselves, they can jump out of danger.

FACT FILE

Scientific name *Gerris lacustris*

Habitat Ponds and still waters

Breeding Male and female mate on the surface of the water and the female lays her eggs on land

Pond skaters avoid freezing to death on ice-covered water by hibernating in the winter. They fly long distances to find a safe resting place until April.

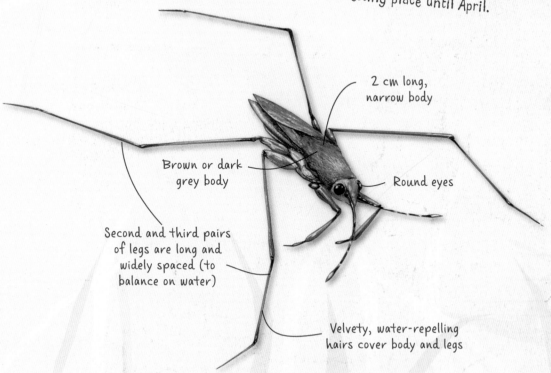

2 cm long, narrow body

Brown or dark grey body

Round eyes

Second and third pairs of legs are long and widely spaced (to balance on water)

Velvety, water-repelling hairs cover body and legs

BLOODY-NOSED BEETLE

Bloody-nosed beetles are widespread in Britain, especially southern areas. However, they are hard to spot because, like many other beetles, they are secretive animals. They can be found in hedgerows or other sheltered areas, and they are most active at night, although they can be seen scuttling around on hot summer days. These large beetles feed on the leaves of low-growing plants and hibernate until April, to avoid the cold winter months when food is in short supply.

FACT FILE

Scientific name
Timarcha tenebricosa

Habitat Woodlands, farms, parks and heaths

Breeding Bluish-black larvae hatch in April, spend the summer eating, then mature into adults

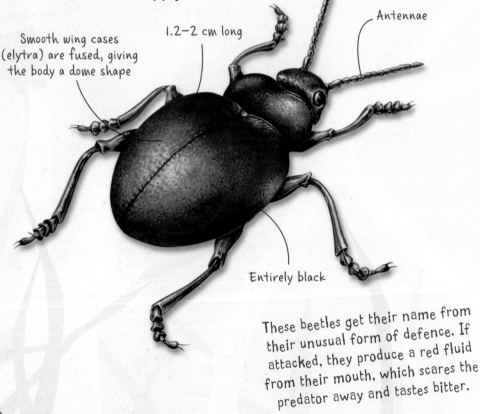

Smooth wing cases (elytra) are fused, giving the body a dome shape

1.2–2 cm long

Antennae

Entirely black

These beetles get their name from their unusual form of defence. If attacked, they produce a red fluid from their mouth, which scares the predator away and tastes bitter.

LADYBIRD

Brightly coloured beetles, ladybirds have round bodies and hard wing cases, called elytra. Adults spend winter in large groups, hidden under loose bark on trees or crammed into crevices. Ladybird larvae hatch from small eggs that are glued to plants either singly or in small groups. They mostly eat other soft-bodied animals. Thirteen-spot and five-spot ladybirds are very rare and seldom seen in the UK. The two-spot ladybird is smaller than its seven-spotted cousin.

FACT FILE

Scientific name
Coccinellidae family

Habitat Gardens and woodlands

Breeding Blue larvae with cream spots

When handled, ladybirds produce drops of smelly yellow fluid from their legs to deter predators. Their bright colours also warn predators to stay away.

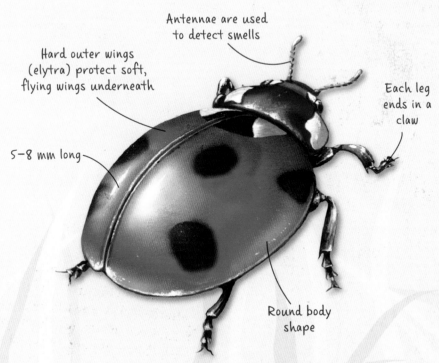

Antennae are used to detect smells

Hard outer wings (elytra) protect soft, flying wings underneath

Each leg ends in a claw

5–8 mm long

Round body shape

CARDINAL BEETLE

These beetles are very distinctive and easy to identify. Their bodies are long, flattened and bright red, and their heads are either black or red. The hard outer casing on their bodies is formed of the forewings, which cover and protect the soft abdomen and second pair of wings underneath. Cardinal beetles fly from May to July and can sometimes be spotted on flowers or resting on tree trunks, particularly at the edges of woodlands.

FACT FILE

Scientific name
Pyrochroa coccinea

Habitat Woodland

Breeding Larvae are yellowish-brown and live under bark

Black-headed cardinal beetles are most common in Wales and the Midlands, but the red-headed cardinal beetle is common throughout Britain.

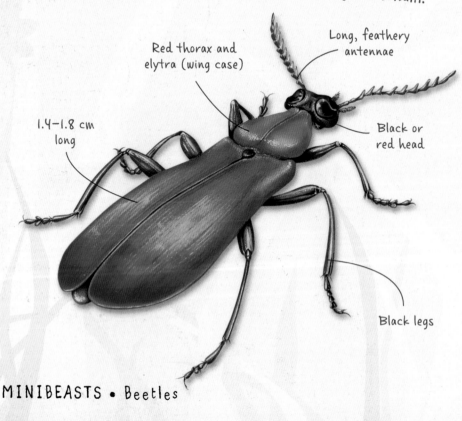

Red thorax and elytra (wing case)

Long, feathery antennae

1.4–1.8 cm long

Black or red head

Black legs

STAG BEETLE

One of the largest and most impressive insects, stag beetles can be heard as they noisily fly at dusk, searching for mates. Adults may only live for a few months and can survive without feeding. Males have large mouthparts called mandibles, which they use to fight one another for females. Gardens with undisturbed areas of rotting wood may attract these endangered animals, as the larvae feed on wood.

FACT FILE

Scientific name
Lucanus cervus

Habitat Woodlands and gardens

Breeding White larvae with brown heads

Stag beetles were common in gardens and parklands, but they have become increasingly rare over the last 50 years and are now threatened with extinction.

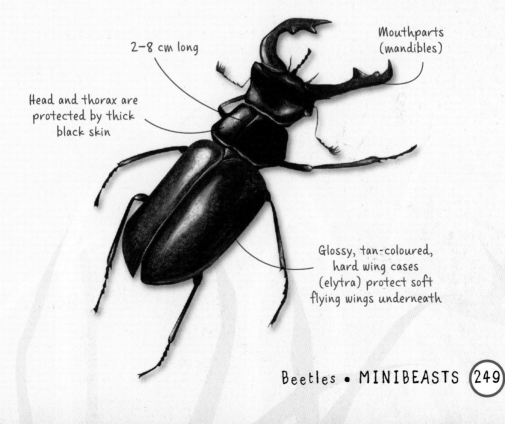

2–8 cm long

Head and thorax are protected by thick black skin

Mouthparts (mandibles)

Glossy, tan-coloured, hard wing cases (elytra) protect soft flying wings underneath

BOMBARDIER BEETLE

Like all ground beetles, bombardier beetles lay their eggs where the newly hatched grubs will find food, such as in a pile of rotting leaves. The grubs grow quickly and moult, or shed, their skin as they get bigger. Eventually they pupate, and during this time of change, the grub grows into an adult beetle. Bombardier beetles cannot fly. To defend themselves from predators, they spray a burning liquid from their rear ends.

FACT FILE

Scientific name
Caribidae family

Habitat Woodlands and gardens

Breeding Larvae are called grubs

The chemicals needed to produce this beetle's burning fluid are stored in the abdomen. They mix together in a special chamber just before being sprayed at a predator.

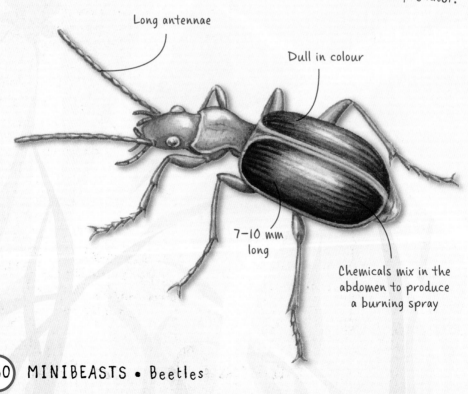

Long antennae

Dull in colour

7–10 mm long

Chemicals mix in the abdomen to produce a burning spray

BRIMSTONE BUTTERFLY

Brimstone butterflies are widespread around Britain and other parts of Europe and North Africa. The bluish-green larvae (caterpillars) feed on buckthorn and alder buckthorn leaves. The adults live on a diet of nectar, which they suck from flowers such as buddleia. Adults emerge from their chrysalises in July and live until the following summer, following a winter hibernation. Females lay their eggs on the underside of buckthorn leaves.

FACT FILE

Scientific name
Gonepteryx rhamni

Habitat Woodland and scrub

Breeding Eggs are laid in May, larvae pupate in June/July and adults emerge two weeks later

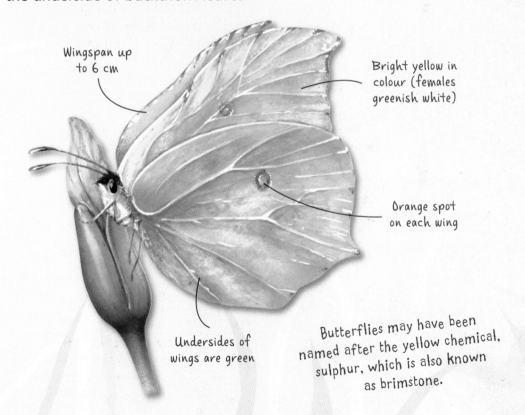

Wingspan up to 6 cm

Bright yellow in colour (females greenish white)

Orange spot on each wing

Undersides of wings are green

Butterflies may have been named after the yellow chemical, sulphur, which is also known as brimstone.

CABBAGE WHITE BUTTERFLY

These are small white, cream or pale yellow butterflies. Females have two black spots on each of their forewings and males have just one. They live in gardens, meadows and fields. Adults suck nectar from flowers, such as dandelions, and the larvae eat leaves of plants from the mustard family, such as cabbage, broccoli and cauliflower. Adults can often be seen in mating rituals, flying upwards in spirals.

FACT FILE

Scientific name *Pieris rapae*

Habitat Gardens and fields

Breeding The larvae are green with black stripes on their backs and sides

Two black spots on each forewing

Soft body covered with bristles

4.5 cm wingspan

Adult butterflies emerge from their pupae in July. They breed twice in summer and the last generation spends winter, protected from cold, as a pupa or chrysalis.

ORANGE TIP BUTTERFLY

These colourful butterflies flit around flowers in early summer, from April to June, laying their eggs. The pale eggs are long and thin, but turn orange after a few days. The green larvae feed on the flower buds, but they will eat each other if they can. The orange tips on the males' forewings warn birds that they taste bad.

FACT FILE

Scientific name
Anthocharis cardamines
Habitat Gardens, meadows and hedgerows
Breeding Lays single eggs

Only one egg is laid at a time, so it can take a female some time to lay her whole clutch on the undersides of flower buds.

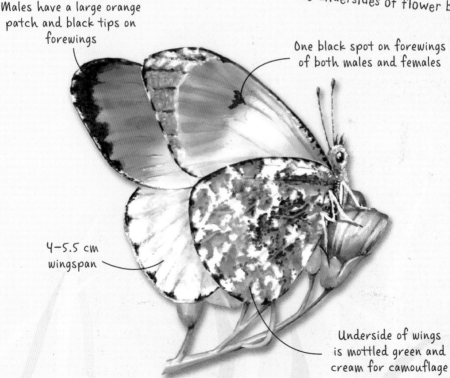

Males have a large orange patch and black tips on forewings

One black spot on forewings of both males and females

4–5.5 cm wingspan

Underside of wings is mottled green and cream for camouflage

HOLLY BLUE BUTTERFLY

Holly blue butterflies are found flying around holly bushes in spring, where females lay their eggs. The larvae, which are small and green, feed on holly flower buds. When they mature, this first brood mates to produce a second brood. This time, the eggs are usually laid on ivy. This second group of adults is able to survive winter as chrysalises, or pupae.

Adult holly blues feed on sap from plants and the sticky substance made by aphids.

3–4 cm wingspan

Antennae have small white stripes

Undersides of wings are pale grey or blue with black spots

Broad black borders to wings in females (narrower in males)

Pale, violet-blue wings

COMMON BLUE BUTTERFLY

These pretty butterflies are most likely to be seen between May and September, when they feed on nectar. They are most common around large, flat-headed flowers, especially near roadsides or meadows. The larvae are green with yellow stripes along their sides and a dark line down their backs. They feed on the leaves of plants, such as white clover and bird's-foot trefoil.

FACT FILE

Scientific name
Polyommatus icarus

Habitat Grasslands, dunes and wastelands

Breeding Larvae are small and green

The larvae produce a substance from their skin that attracts ants, and in turn, the ants protect the larvae from predators.

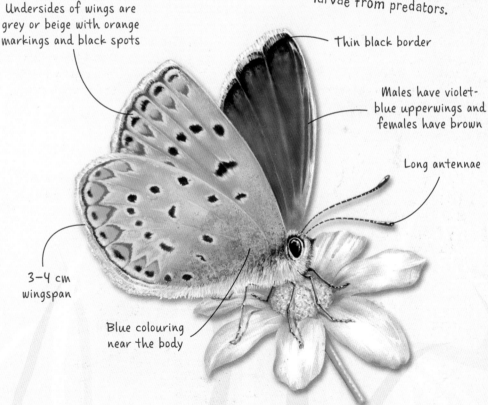

Undersides of wings are grey or beige with orange markings and black spots

Thin black border

Males have violet-blue upperwings and females have brown

Long antennae

3–4 cm wingspan

Blue colouring near the body

PEACOCK BUTTERFLY

Peacock butterflies are often seen on **buddleia in summer.** They wake from hibernation in spring and soon mate. Females lay small green eggs in batches of up to 500, often on nettles or hops, the larvae's favourite food. Adults emerge from the pupae in July and feed on nectar from flowers, or suck the juice from over-ripe fruit. The life expectancy of adults is one year.

FACT FILE

Scientific name *Inachis io*

Habitat Flowery gardens and meadows

Breeding Fully grown larvae are about 4 cm long and they have black-and-white spots and long, black dorsal spines

Peacock butterflies get their name from the large, eyelike patterns on their wings, which are similar to the eye-shaped patterns on the tails of peacock birds.

Long antennae used for smelling and touching

Hair on thorax

5–7.5 cm wingspan

Four false eyes on wings

Dark brown wing edges

COMMA BUTTERFLY

With dull patterns on the underside of their wings, commas can be difficult to see among dead leaves. This camouflage helps to protect the butterflies from predators, such as birds and bats, when they overwinter and hang from leaves. Commas live in gardens, hedges and woodlands. There they can find flowers that supply them with nectar as adults, and leaves such as stinging nettles, which provide food for larvae.

FACT FILE

Scientific name
Polygonia c-album

Habitat Gardens and meadows

Breeding Two broods each year

The larvae are black with red-and-white markings, giving them the appearance of bird droppings. They are covered in spines.

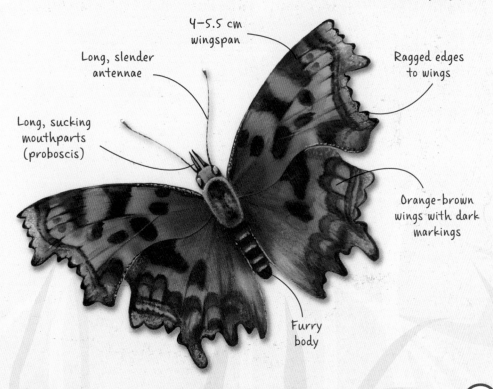

4–5.5 cm wingspan

Long, slender antennae

Long, sucking mouthparts (proboscis)

Ragged edges to wings

Orange-brown wings with dark markings

Furry body

RED ADMIRAL BUTTERFLY

Named after their 'admirable' colours, these butterflies are easily recognized by their dark-coloured wings with red bands and white spots. They have hints of blue and black spots on their hindwings. Red admirals are fast, powerful flyers and – unusually for butterflies – may fly at night. These insects are found throughout the UK and Europe and inhabit gardens, parks, woodlands, seashores and mountains.

FACT FILE

Scientific name
Vanessa atalanta

Habitat Gardens and meadows

Breeding Eggs are laid singularly on nettle leaves

The larvae of red admirals are normally dark and bristled, but the colour varies from green–grey–black with yellow lines on either side.

Red bands on forewings

Long antennae

6 cm wingspan

Red patches along the back of hindwings

Edges of wings lined with blue spots

SMALL TORTOISESHELL BUTTERFLY

Named after their colouring, small tortoiseshells are often one of the first types of butterfly to be seen in spring. Adults emerge from hibernation in March or April and mate soon afterwards. They lay their eggs on food plants, such as nettles, and they hatch about ten days later. Small tortoiseshells are common butterflies and live in a range of habitats, particularly near human homes.

FACT FILE

Scientific name *Aglais urticae*

Habitat Flowery gardens and meadows

Breeding Heaps of eggs are laid on the underside of nettle leaves in April

This butterfly's Latin name, *Aglais urticae*, comes from the word for nettles, *urtica*, the butterfly's favourite food.

Blue markings along wing edges

4–5.5 cm wingspan

Points on the edges of forewings and hindwings

Orange-and-black markings on wings

SPECKLED WOOD BUTTERFLY

Speckled wood butterflies fly around woodlands and gardens in the summer months. They do not surround flowers (like many other butterflies do) because they do not feed on nectar, but on the sugary substance that aphids make. Females lay single eggs on grasses, which the larvae feed on when they hatch. The larvae eat and moult for about ten days before turning into chrysalises.

FACT FILE

Scientific name
Pararge aegeria

Habitat Woodlands and gardens

Breeding Larvae are green

Males fiercely defend their territories from rival males. They can sometimes be seen fighting, with their wings clashing.

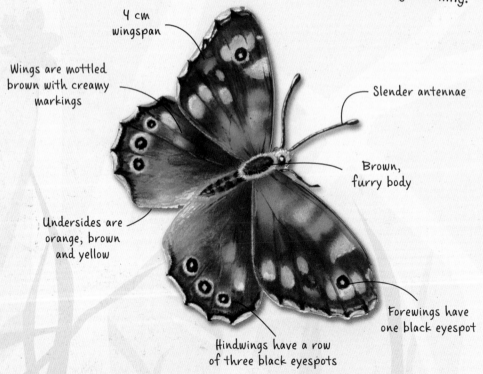

4 cm wingspan

Wings are mottled brown with creamy markings

Slender antennae

Brown, furry body

Undersides are orange, brown and yellow

Forewings have one black eyespot

Hindwings have a row of three black eyespots

SWALLOWTAIL BUTTERFLY

Swallowtails are Britain's largest butterflies and among the most attractive. Their name describes the long 'tails' that grow at the back of the hindwings. The larvae are black and white and resemble bird droppings, which protects them from predators. As they grow, they turn green and black, with orange marks, and produce a foul smell to keep predators at bay. The adults feed on nectar and the larvae feed only on milk parsley.

Swallowtails were once common in many British marshlands, but are now found only in the marshes around the Norfolk Broads.

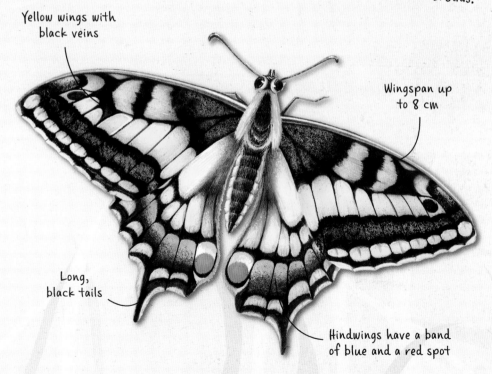

Yellow wings with black veins

Wingspan up to 8 cm

Long, black tails

Hindwings have a band of blue and a red spot

GARDEN TIGER MOTH

Garden tiger moths are very common and easy to spot with their bold colours. The red-coloured hindwings warn other animals that they taste bad and to leave them alone. Garden tigers feed on nectar from flowers. The larvae are brown and black, and are so hairy they have been given the name of 'woolly bears'. The hairs cause irritation, so they protect the larvae from hungry birds.

FACT FILE

Scientific name *Arctia caja*
Habitat Gardens, farms and open areas
Breeding Black and orange larvae

Garden tiger moths are variable in appearance and it is rare to find two moths with exactly the same markings.

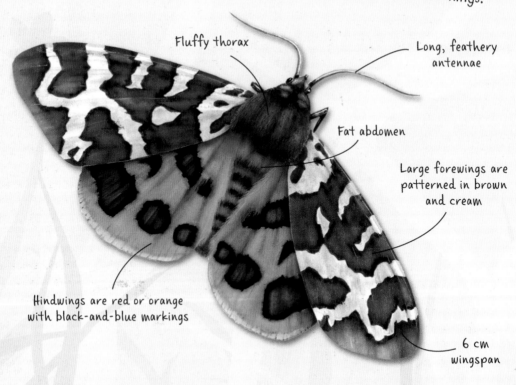

Fluffy thorax

Long, feathery antennae

Fat abdomen

Large forewings are patterned in brown and cream

Hindwings are red or orange with black-and-blue markings

6 cm wingspan

MAGPIE MOTH

Boldly patterned, magpie moths have black-and-white wings with yellow bands. This colouring warns predators, such as birds and spiders, that they taste foul. The adults emerge from their pupae in June and drink nectar from flowers. They can be seen until August and, unlike many other moths, they are active during the day.

FACT FILE

Scientific name
Abraxas grossulariata

Habitat Meadows and woods

Breeding Larvae feed on various shrubs

Forewings are white with black bands and spots

Long antennae

4–5 cm wingspan

Orange band crosses the forewings

Moths and butterflies belong to the same insect family. However moths usually have drab colours, are active at night and have thick or feathery antennae.

DEATH'S HEAD HAWK-MOTH

This striking species of moth gets its name from the unusual pattern on the back of its thorax. This is the part of the body between the head and the fleshy abdomen. The pattern resembles a skull, which is also known as a 'death's head'. These moths are not native to Britain, but migrate here for summer. The larvae feed on potato plants, so the adults are more likely to be found in farms than in woods or gardens.

FACT FILE

Scientific name
Acherontia atropos

Habitat Farmland

Breeding The pale green larvae have purple and white stripes, and can grow up to 15 cm in length

These moths have the strange habit of crawling into beehives in search of honey. They can produce a loud squeaking noise if they are handled or startled.

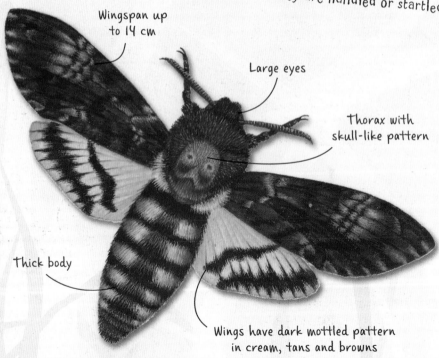

Wingspan up to 14 cm

Large eyes

Thorax with skull-like pattern

Thick body

Wings have dark mottled pattern in cream, tans and browns

CODLING MOTH

The larvae of the codling moth are pests that eat the fruit of some trees, particularly apple and pear. Adult females lay a single egg on a leaf of the tree. When the larva emerges, it bores into apples or pears, making long tunnels as it eats its way through the fruit flesh. The larva pupates under bark or in leaf litter, emerging as an adult between November and February, depending on the weather conditions.

FACT FILE

Scientific name
Cydia pomonella

Habitat Where apple trees grow

Breeding Larvae are also known as apple maggots and they have white bodies and brown heads

The large eye-shaped markings on the tips of the codling moth's forewings distract and confuse predators, such as birds.

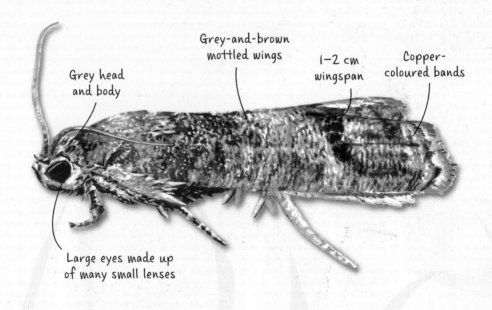

Grey-and-brown mottled wings

1–2 cm wingspan

Copper-coloured bands

Grey head and body

Large eyes made up of many small lenses

CENTIPEDE & MILLIPEDE

These bugs aren't actually insects, but belong to a group of creatures called **myriapods.** Centipedes and millipedes have long bodies that are divided into many segments. Centipedes have one pair of legs on each segment, while millipedes have two. The number of segments varies. The common centipede is chestnut-brown in colour and adults have 15 pairs of legs. They hunt for insects, slugs and worms at night. Flat-backed millipedes live in compost heaps and leaf litter.

FACT FILE

Scientific name
Centipede *Chilopoda* superclass
Millipede *Diplopoda* superclass

Habitat Leaf litter and soil

Breeding Larvae moult and
grow many times

The world's largest centipedes, scolopendrids, live in South America. They measure up to 30 cm in length and use their venomous claws to catch mice and frogs.

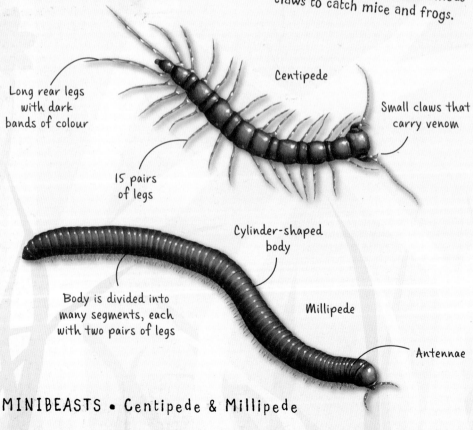

Long rear legs
with dark
bands of colour

Centipede

Small claws that
carry venom

15 pairs
of legs

Cylinder-shaped
body

Body is divided into
many segments, each
with two pairs of legs

Millipede

Antennae

HARVESTMAN

With eight legs, harvestmen belong to the same group of animals as spiders and scorpions – the arachnids. Unlike spiders, their bodies are rounded, without a waist. Females are usually bigger than males, and can lay 20–100 eggs at a time. Their long, skinny legs end in tiny claws and their small mouthparts can produce foul substances to keep predators away. They feed at night, mostly on small invertebrates (animals without backbones).

FACT FILE

Scientific name
Phalangium opilio

Habitat Thick vegetation

Breeding Young are small, but fully formed

Harvestmen do not have spinnerets for secreting silk thread to make nests and webs. They also lack venom glands and do not have a poisonous bite.

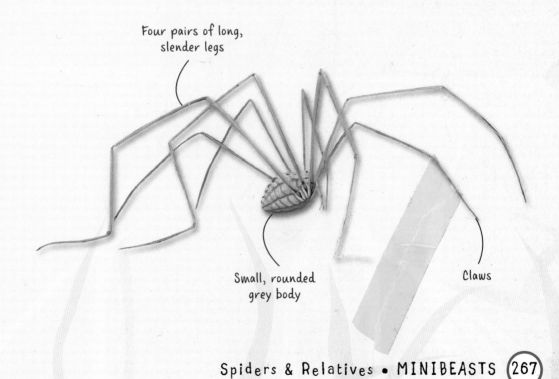

Four pairs of long, slender legs

Small, rounded grey body

Claws

GARDEN SPIDER

These spiders are usually brown, beige and black in colour, although patterns do vary. There are mottled white patches on the abdomen, which often look like a cross. Females are about twice the size of males. Garden spiders are common in meadows, farms, woodlands and gardens. They spin silk, which they use to build their webs and to make cocoons to protect their eggs.

FACT FILE

Scientific name
Araneus diadematus

Habitat Gardens, parks and woodlands

Breeding Young are small, but fully-formed spiders

Spiders usually have eight eyes, eight legs, and are venomous. Their bodies are divided into two main segments — the cephalothorax and the abdomen.

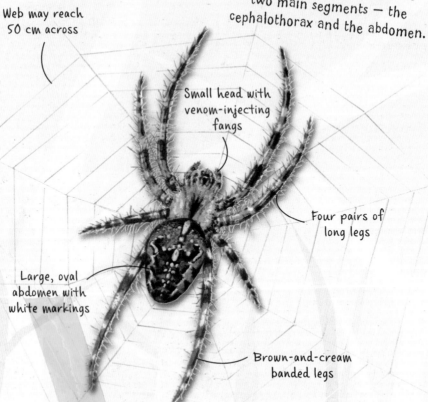

Web may reach 50 cm across

Small head with venom-injecting fangs

Four pairs of long legs

Large, oval abdomen with white markings

Brown-and-cream banded legs

WASP SPIDER

The distinctive wasp spider is easy to identify, with its bold pattern of stripes. This banding may deter predators, such as birds, which think the stripes signify a sting or poison. However, it is only seen on females, which are more colourful than the dull males, and much bigger too. Wasp spiders prey on flying insects and grasshoppers, which they catch in their orb webs. They wrap their captured prey in silk before devouring them.

FACT FILE

Scientific name
Argiope bruennichi

Habitat Grasslands, gardens and coasts

Breeding After mating with a female, the male has to escape her clutches or risk being eaten

Wasp spiders live in southern areas, as they actually come from Mediterranean countries. If global warming continues, they may move further north.

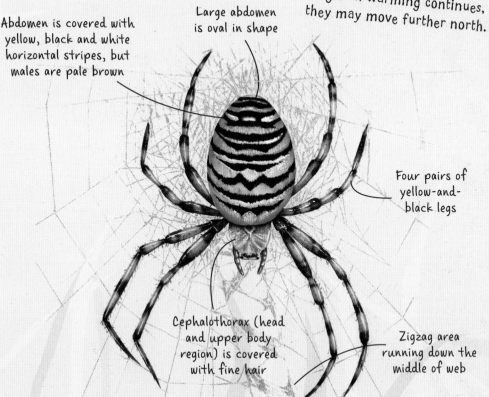

Abdomen is covered with yellow, black and white horizontal stripes, but males are pale brown

Large abdomen is oval in shape

Four pairs of yellow-and-black legs

Cephalothorax (head and upper body region) is covered with fine hair

Zigzag area running down the middle of web

CHAMOMILE

This daisy-like plant is best known for its delicious scent, which is like a mixture of apples and bubblegum. Chamomile used to be widespread, but many of its natural habitats have been destroyed. It is now found growing wild in only a few places in the south of England, especially the New Forest.

FACT FILE

Scientific name
Chamaemelum nobile

Type Daisy family

Size 25 cm

Flowers June to August

Fruit Small seeds

Flower is about 2 cm across

One flower head on each stalk

Chamomile often grows as a ground-covering plant, and is used to create chamomile lawns, which release their scent when walked on.

Large yellow disc contains many florets

Petals dip down

Grey-green feathery leaves

DAISY

The tiny white flowers that pepper garden lawns are called daisies and they are often regarded as weeds. The name, daisy, comes from 'day's eye' because the flower opens like an eye when the sun comes out. Daisies attract pollinating insects, such as bees and hoverflies. Their leaves are hairy and shaped like spoons, and the attractive flowers grow out of the centre of the plant. The plants survive cold and wet winters, and flower from spring onwards. The flowers grow upwards, facing the sun.

FACT FILE

Scientific name
Bellis perennis

Type Perennial flower

Size 2–10 cm

Flowers Small white flowers appear all summer

Fruit Tiny seeds, after flowering

Dried daisy flowers are used in traditional remedies for treating coughs and colds, diseases of the joints and minor wounds.

Underside of petals are tinged with deep pink

Small, oval-shaped petals surround yellow disc

Straight, 'hairy' stem

OXEYE DAISY

Oxeye daisies are common in meadows, where their bright, bold flower heads catch the eye. They grow from year to year, and spread widely to create a carpet of green, topped with white-and-yellow flower heads. Common daisies look similar to these flowers, but they have smooth, oval leaves and only grow to about 10 cm in height.

FACT FILE

Scientific name
Leucanthemum vulgare

Type Daisy family

Size 10–80 cm

Flowers May to September

Fruit Small seeds

Fritillary butterflies flock to oxeye daisies in summer. Their wings have orange–brown markings on the upper surfaces, and paler undersides.

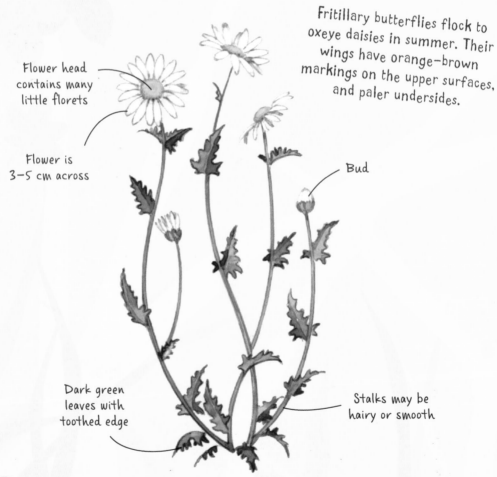

Flower head contains many little florets

Flower is 3–5 cm across

Bud

Dark green leaves with toothed edge

Stalks may be hairy or smooth

MEADOWSWEET

Meadowsweet has clouds of whitish flowers on tall stems and has a strong perfume. It is popular with flying insects, and thrives in grasslands throughout Britain and Ireland. Long ago, the blooms were scattered over floors to make a house smell sweet.

Meadowsweet keeps blooming throughout the whole summer, providing food for many insects. Its sweet nectar particularly attracts butterflies and bees.

Flower is about 5 mm across

Creamy-white flowers

Dark green leaves, pale underneath

Hairless, reddish stems

WATER-PLANTAIN

You can see the flowers of this plant best in the afternoon, because they are only open between around 1 p.m. and 7 p.m. every day. Water-plantain is a stout plant that grows on the edges of watery habitats, especially ponds. It is found everywhere, except northern Scotland.

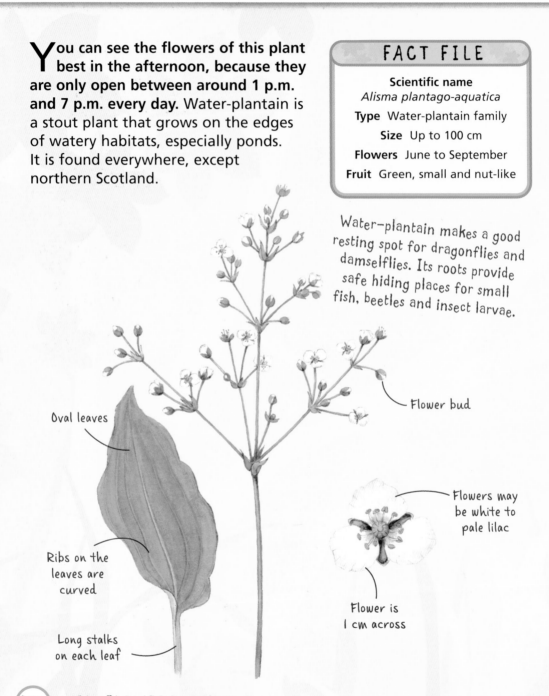

FACT FILE

Scientific name
Alisma plantago-aquatica

Type Water-plantain family

Size Up to 100 cm

Flowers June to September

Fruit Green, small and nut-like

Water-plantain makes a good resting spot for dragonflies and damselflies. Its roots provide safe hiding places for small fish, beetles and insect larvae.

Flower bud

Oval leaves

Ribs on the leaves are curved

Long stalks on each leaf

Flowers may be white to pale lilac

Flower is 1 cm across

WOOD ANEMONE

Wood anemones come into flower in spring, so they decorate woodland floors before many trees have unfurled their leaves. These flowers are able to move towards the light, so they follow the sun as it moves through the sky. Although they have a slight scent, wood anemones do not contain nectar, so insects visiting the flowers may leave hungry.

FACT FILE

Scientific name
Anemone nemorosa

Type Buttercup family

Size Up to 30 cm

Flowers March and April

Fruit Clusters of seeds on old flower head

Wood anemones are found in the same habitats as bluebells, which also come into flower during spring. Look out for them together, as they look beautiful on a woodland floor.

Each flower has five to ten petals

Flower is about 2.5 cm across

Long stalks on leaves

Each leaf has three lobes

Petals (which are actually sepals) have a pinkish hue

BINDWEED

Although its white, trumpet-shaped flowers attract pollinating insects, bindweed is often an unwelcome addition to gardens. It is a weed that grows widely, climbing up fences and plants, gradually smothering them. Bindweed gets into gardens when plants are brought in, or through compost and manure. It can also spread by seed and is almost impossible to remove. Even a tiny piece of root can grow into a new plant.

FACT FILE

Scientific name
Convolvulus arvensis

Type Perennial weed

Size 50–200 cm

Flowers White or pink trumpets, from May to September

Fruit Seeds, August to October

Bindweed roots are fleshy and white. They grow extensively underground, and may grow down 5 m or more, making it very difficult to get rid of the weed.

Large heart-shaped green leaves

Long, white flower buds

Trumpet-shaped flowers with no scent

Twining, slender stems

Green outer leaves protect flower bud

BROAD-LEAVED HELLEBORINE

The broad-leaved helleborine is a striking plant, with a single spike that grows tall, bearing up to 100 flowers. Its delicately coloured petals are similar to those of other orchids, and are perfectly shaped to put pollen on the back of any visiting bees. Wasps can be seen feeding on the nectar, and ants often climb into the cup-shaped flowers.

FACT FILE

Scientific name
Epipactis helleborine

Type Orchid family

Size Up to 90 cm

Flowers July to September

Fruit Pear-shaped

Red helleborines usually grow in shady places. These wild flowers are extremely rare, and are found in only a few places in southern England.

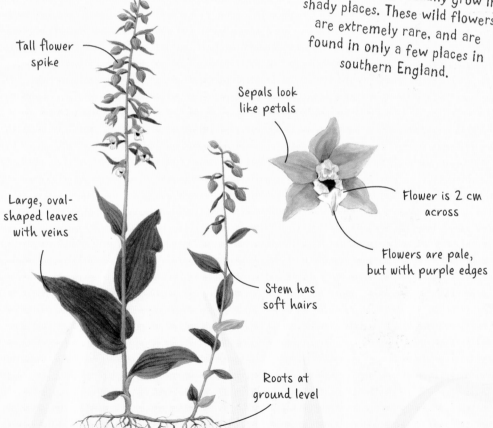

Tall flower spike

Large, oval-shaped leaves with veins

Sepals look like petals

Flower is 2 cm across

Flowers are pale, but with purple edges

Stem has soft hairs

Roots at ground level

LORDS & LADIES

The flowers from a lords and ladies plant produce a strong, unpleasant smell that attracts insects, which crawl into the flower heads looking for nectar. As they search, the insects rub against the pollen in the male flowers, and fertilize the female ones. Insects may get trapped and die, and their bodies can be seen in the spathe.

Thick leaf, called a spathe, which protects the growing flower

Rower-bearing stalk, called the spadix

Spadix is 5 cm tall

Large, arrow-shaped leaves

If the spathe is cut open the flowers can be seen growing on the spadix. The female flowers are at the base and darker male flowers grow just above them.

Red berries

Stiff, upright stem

IVY

This shrub is usually grown in gardens as decorative cover, to hide fences and walls, or to provide a lush green carpet beneath trees where little else grows. There are many different types of ivy, but most of them have glossy, heart-shaped leaves. Shoots grow in all directions and many of them have tough roots to anchor new stems to the ground, or any other good growing surface.

FACT FILE

Scientific name *Hedera*

Type Evergreen shrub

Size Up to 30 m

Flowers Small, yellow-green, from late autumn onwards

Fruit Small black berries, from winter onwards

Although the ivy's black berries are an important food source for birds, they are extremely poisonous to humans.

Small, black berries

Woody stem

Stems are covered in tiny roots that grow into soil, walls or fences

Flat leaves are dark green and glossy

HONEYSUCKLE

A climbing bush, honeysuckle is often found creeping up walls and fences. Its pretty flowers have an unusual shape, but even more distinctive is the strong scent they produce. The nectar from these flowers attracts many insect visitors to the garden, including bees and butterflies. Honeysuckle grows quickly, producing many tendrils that cover fences, walls and trees. The leaves are favoured by many caterpillars and they often pupate (change from larva to pupa) among them.

FACT FILE

Scientific name *Lonicera japonica*
Type Evergreen/deciduous shrub
Size Up to 10 m
Flowers Mainly white or yellow, from spring to summer
Fruit Red, blue or black berries containing seeds, from late summer to autumn

The flowers and dried leaves of the Japanese honeysuckle, *Lonicera japonica*, have been used for many centuries in traditional Chinese medicine.

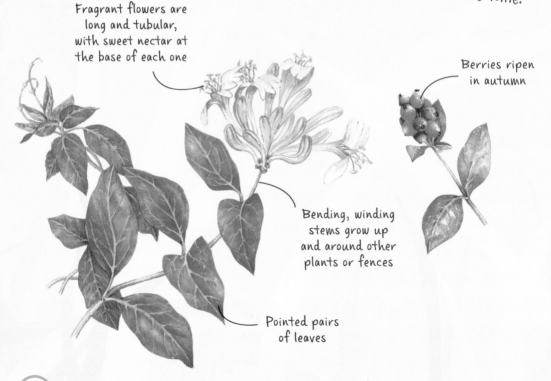

Fragrant flowers are long and tubular, with sweet nectar at the base of each one

Berries ripen in autumn

Bending, winding stems grow up and around other plants or fences

Pointed pairs of leaves

BEE ORCHID

There are around 40 members of the wild orchid family in England and Wales, and bee orchids are one of the best known and most widespread of them. Each stem holds between two and seven flowers, and each flower looks as if a fat bumblebee has settled on it. Bee orchids are probably extinct in Scotland.

FACT FILE

Scientific name *Orphrys apifera*
Type Orchid family
Size Up to 30 cm
Flowers June and July
Fruit Long and green with ridges

The lower petal of this orchid looks like a bee. Male bees are attracted to it, and as they settle on the flower their backs are coated in pollen.

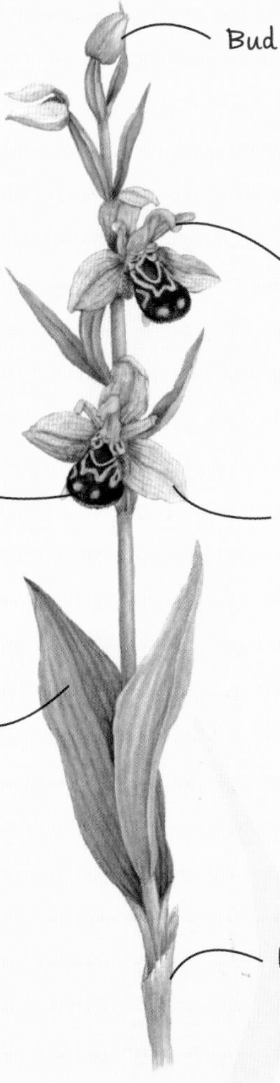

Bud
Upper petals are rolled, like cylinders, often green or brown
Central lobe of lower petal feels like velvet
Flower is 4 cm, from top to bottom
Leaves are pointed and slender
Leafy stem

CROSS-LEAVED HEATH

This evergreen plant keeps its leaves all year round. They are arranged in a circle, called a whorl, around the stem. Cross-leaved heath has pretty pink flowers, which hang like bells. They stay on the plant until late summer, making a colourful display in boggy places, and attract bees.

FACT FILE

Scientific name *Erica tetralix*

Type Heather family

Size Up to 30 cm

Flowers July to September

Fruit Small, downy, dark brown capsules

Pink flowers droop

Many flowers in each cluster

Heathers such as the cross-leaved heath tend to keep their leaves over the winter. Their flowers are usually small and bell-like.

Narrow, sticky leaves, with hairs

Whorls of four leaves arranged around the stem

Small leaves

Egg-shaped flower

Flower is 6 mm long

DEPTFORD PINK

The colour of this flower's petals is often described as cerise, and its stem is greyish. Deptford pinks are biennial, which means that their life cycle takes two years. This plant produces up to 400 seeds at the end of the summer. A round clump, or rosette, of leaves grows the following year, and flowers bloom the year after that.

FACT FILE

Scientific name
Dianthus armeria

Type Pink family

Size Up to 60 cm

Flowers June to August

Fruit Small capsules

Sweet williams are related to Deptford pinks, and are popular in gardens. Their flowers are larger than those of Deptford pinks, and grow in a range of colours.

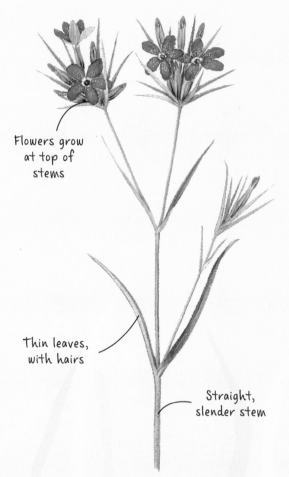

Flowers grow at top of stems

Thin leaves, with hairs

Straight, slender stem

Five petals

FOXGLOVE

This flower is easy to spot, with its tall spikes that are covered in up to 80 pink flowers. The plant gets its name from the tube-shaped flowers, which are said to resemble little gloves for a fox. The large, pale green leaves are soft on top and woolly underneath.

FACT FILE

Scientific name
Digitalis purpurea

Type Digitalis family

Size 40–150 cm

Flowers June to August

Fruit Green capsules

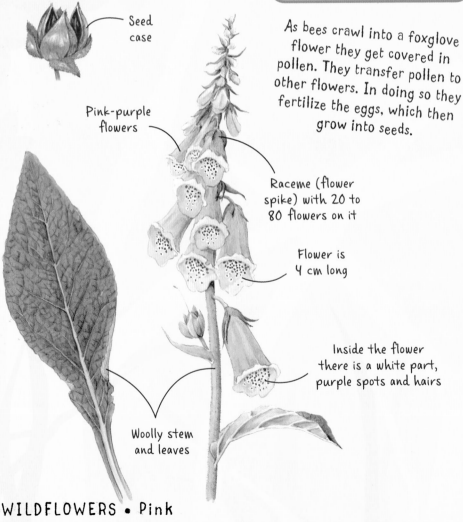

Seed case

Pink-purple flowers

As bees crawl into a foxglove flower they get covered in pollen. They transfer pollen to other flowers. In doing so they fertilize the eggs, which then grow into seeds.

Raceme (flower spike) with 20 to 80 flowers on it

Flower is 4 cm long

Inside the flower there is a white part, purple spots and hairs

Woolly stem and leaves

GREAT WILLOWHERB

Willowherbs are unusually tall wildflowers, so it is easy to find them in damp places throughout Britain, except the far northwest, where they rarely grow. They can come from seeds, but they also spread out by fattened roots, called rhizomes, in the soil. This can lead to a large, colourful clump forming in one spot.

FACT FILE

Scientific name
Epilobium hirsutum

Type Onagraceae family

Size Up to 200 cm

Flowers July and August

Fruit Soft pods contain airborne seeds

These flowers are called codlins-and-cream because they are pink and white. Codlins were rosy apples that were boiled in milk and served with cream.

Flowerless stalk

Rosy-pink petals attract bees and hoverflies

Flower is 25 mm across

Creamy-white stigma

Long, narrow leaves, pointed

Woolly stems and leaves

HEATHER

You can find heather in both damp and dry places. It grows into bushes with many branches and each bush can reach 100 cm tall and 100 cm wide. Heather keeps its leaves over the winter, and its flowers, which are sometimes white, can last from spring to autumn.

FACT FILE

Scientific name
Calluna vulgaris

Type Heather family

Size 50–100 cm

Flowers July to September

Fruit Capsules

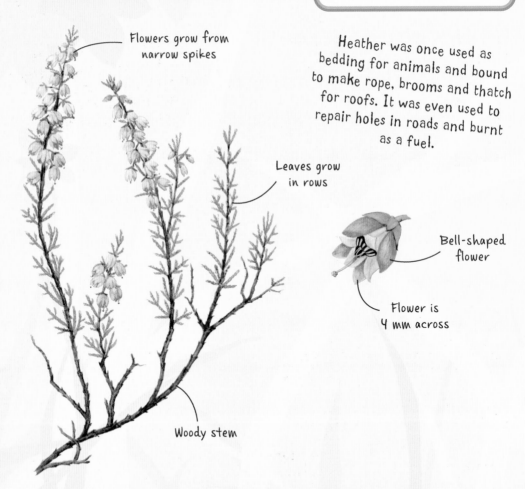

Flowers grow from
narrow spikes

Heather was once used as bedding for animals and bound to make rope, brooms and thatch for roofs. It was even used to repair holes in roads and burnt as a fuel.

Leaves grow
in rows

Bell-shaped
flower

Flower is
4 mm across

Woody stem

HERB-ROBERT

Herb-Robert is a survivor. It can live in sun or shade, and can cope with mild winter weather, unlike many other wildflowers that die down after the summer. As Herb-Robert is not fussy about the type of soil it lives in, it is common throughout Britain.

Herb-Robert turns red in the autumn. Although it is very pretty, this plant can quickly take over an area, killing off weaker plants that cannot reach the light.

Five petals on a flower, can be pink or white

Flower is 12 mm across

Seed case

Feathery leaves

Red stems, hairy and oily

INDIAN BALSAM

Indian balsam was introduced to Britain in 1839, having been brought from the Himalayan mountain region. It is one of the tallest wildflowers, and is seen all over Britain, especially in England and Wales. The flowers produce lots of nectar, so there are likely to be bees, wasps and other insects nearby.

FACT FILE

Scientific name
Impatiens glandulifera

Type Often treated as a weed

Size 100–200 cm

Flowers July to October

Fruit Explosive seed pods

In some places, Indian balsam is called 'bee-bums', because when a bee is exploring inside the flower, feeding on nectar, all you can see is its tail end!

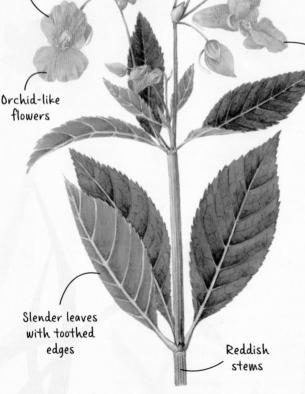

Flower is 3 cm across

Orchid-like flowers

Petals are pink or occasionally white

Explosive seed pod

Slender leaves with toothed edges

Reddish stems

PURPLE-LOOSESTRIFE

Purple-loosestrife plants often grow close together in wet places, with their magenta-pink flower spikes standing tall above the green leaves. These plants are perennial, which means they can live for more than two years before dying down, and the flowers last for the whole summer.

Clumps of purple-loosestrife attract many types of wildlife, including bumblebees, honeybees, brimstone butterflies and elephant hawk-moths.

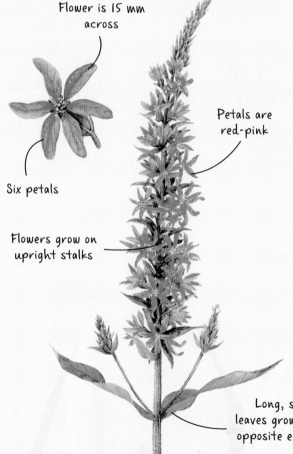

Flower is 15 mm across

Petals are red-pink

Six petals

Flowers grow on upright stalks

Long, slender leaves grow in pairs, opposite each other

RED CAMPION

The flowers of red campion are mostly pink rather than red. There are five petals on each flower head, but it can look as if there are more when the petals are very deeply lobed. The flowers are visited by bumblebees, butterflies and moths, which feed on the sweet nectar.

FACT FILE

Scientific name
Silene dioica

Type Pink family

Size Up to 100 cm

Flowers March to October

Fruit Round, dry capsule

Red campion blooms as bluebells are finishing. Woodlands with wood anemones, bluebells and red campion go through shades of white, blue and pink from spring to autumn.

Pink petals, occasionally with red tips

Flower is up to 25 mm across

Seed capsule

Long, hairy stems, slightly sticky

Oval hairy leaves in pairs

THRIFT

Thrift has candyfloss flower heads growing above a dense mat of leaves. It is an unusual plant that can grow in very dry places, especially at the coast. The clump of leaves makes a safe home for beetles and other insects, and bees visit the pink flowers. When many clumps grow together, they create a cushion of soft leaves.

FACT FILE

Scientific name
Armeria maritima

Type Thrift family

Size Up to 20 cm

Flowers April to October

Fruit Capsules

According to folklore, if you have thrift in your garden you will never be poor. Named after the practice of taking care of your money, it was depicted on the back of an old English coin.

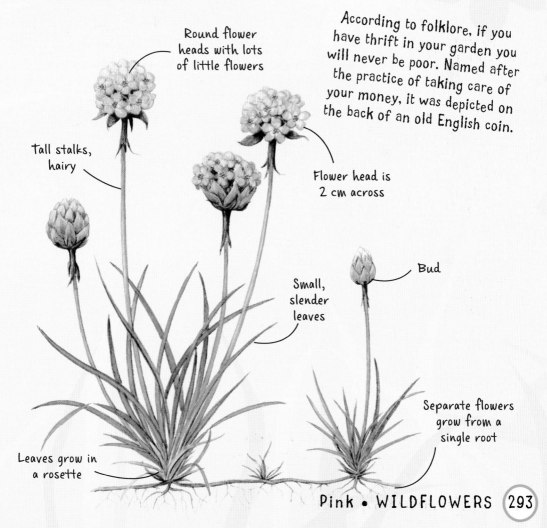

Round flower heads with lots of little flowers

Tall stalks, hairy

Flower head is 2 cm across

Bud

Small, slender leaves

Leaves grow in a rosette

Separate flowers grow from a single root

MARSH CINQUEFOIL

The deep pink or red flowers of the Marsh cinquefoil are unlike any other flower. They are star shaped, and grow at the top of upright magenta-coloured stems. There are five sepals and smaller purple petals form a layer on top of them. Other cinquefoils, which grow in dry places, have yellow flowers and are not star shaped.

FACT FILE

Scientific name
Potentilla palustris

Type Rose family

Size 20–50 cm

Flowers June and July

Fruit Dry, small and papery

Although the flower of this plant is very distinctive, you can still recognize it when it is not in bloom by its large, toothed leaves, which are mostly divided into five leaflets.

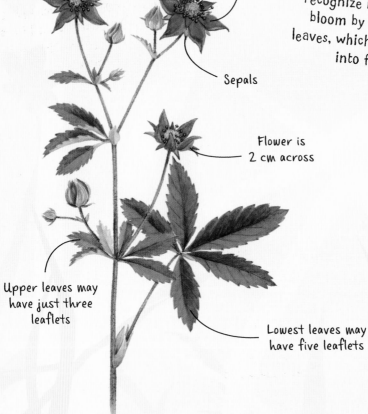

Petals

Sepals

Flower is 2 cm across

Upper leaves may have just three leaflets

Lowest leaves may have five leaflets

PHEASANT'S EYE

Pheasant's eye is a type of buttercup, with five to eight glossy scarlet petals and feathery leaves. By August the flowers are dying down to be replaced by large seed cases. When the seeds fall to the ground they may rest there – they are described as 'dormant' – until the following spring, or even several years later.

FACT FILE

Scientific name
Adonis annua

Type Buttercup family

Size Up to 40 cm

Flowers June to August

Fruit Large and wrinkled

This flower is rare, as each plant only produces a few heavy seeds that are not easily transported to new areas. It has also been killed off in many areas by the use of chemicals.

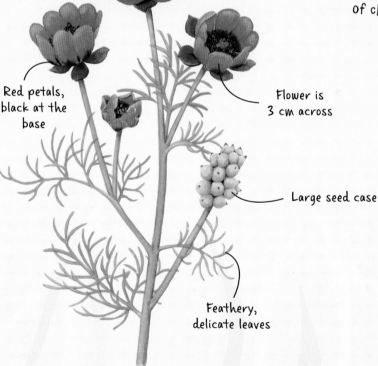

Black centre

Red petals, black at the base

Flower is 3 cm across

Large seed case

Feathery, delicate leaves

POPPY

The scarlet, papery petals of the poppy are often black at the base. The flowers grow at the top of a long, hairy stalk. The leaves are distinctive, with their feathery appearance and toothed edges.

FACT FILE

Scientific name
Papaver rhoeas

Type Poppy family

Size 40–80 cm

Flowers June to August

Fruit Round capsule

Four petals

Flower is 7 cm across

Poppies are common in farmers' fields because they grow particularly well on soil that has been disturbed, and they can flower and seed themselves before the farmer's crop is harvested.

Seed head droops

Hairy stalks

Long slender leaves, divided to give a feathery appearance

Tough seed case

SCARLET PIMPERNEL

It is easy to overlook the tiny red flowers of the scarlet pimpernel. These plants are small and grow low to the ground, with the stems sprawling out along the soil. Purple hairs inside the flower attract many insects in summer. Scarlet pimpernels are common throughout Britain, but are mostly found near the coast in Scotland.

The petals of scarlet pimpernel close when air pressure drops — a sign that rain might be due. It can also be used to tell the time, as petals open in the morning and close mid-afternoon.

Bright scarlet flowers

Flower is 12 mm across

Egg-shaped leaves

Creeping stems

Black dots on underside of leaves

BLUEBELL

These plants normally bear blue flowers, but there are violet, pink and white ones, too. Flower spikes grow from a clump of deep green leaves. Each spike bears four to 16 bell-shaped flowers in clusters. Bluebells were once common, but many bluebell woods have been damaged by people picking the flowers and digging up the bulbs.

FACT FILE

Scientific name
Hyacinthoides non-scripta

Type Lily family

Size 10–40 cm

Flowers April to June

Fruit Capsules

Beautiful bluebells carpet woodland floors in spring, creating a stunning sight. Visitors like to enjoy the floral display and strong fragrance.

Flower spikes (racemes) are upright when in bud

As the flowers open they droop, like bells

Flower is 15 mm long

Papery seed case

Strong, long and glossy leaves

BROOKLIME

Brooklime is a creeping plant that produces stems that grow along the ground. Roots grow from these stems at places called nodes. The flowering stems grow upright and produce star-shaped blooms throughout the summer. The petals are usually blue, but pink ones grow, too, and there is a white 'eye' in the centre of each bloom.

FACT FILE

Scientific name
Veronica beccabunga

Type Water plant of the Speedwell family

Size Up to 30 cm

Flowers May to September

Fruit Round flat capsules

Brooklime grows in wet ground and in water. Its leaves and stems provide shelter for small pond-living animals such as insects, sticklebacks (small fish) and tadpoles.

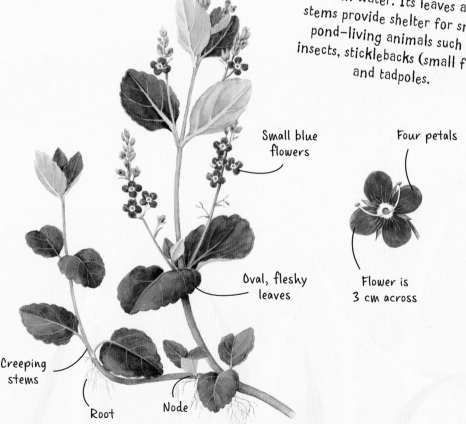

Small blue flowers

Four petals

Oval, fleshy leaves

Flower is 3 cm across

Creeping stems

Root

Node

BUGLE

Bugle forms dense mats of green
leaves, covering the ground. Flower
stems grow upwards and bear clusters
of many small, purple flowers.
Occasionally, the flowers are pink or
white. Bugle leaves are unusual because
they have a dark green background
colour, with a purple sheen. Butterflies
often flitter around this plant and feed
on it.

FACT FILE

Scientific name
Ajuga reptans

Type Dead-nettle family

Size Up to 20 cm

Flowers April to June

Fruit Nutlets

This plant grows throughout
Britain. In some places it is
called carpenter's herb, because it
was once used to stop bleeding
and people often grew it in their
gardens for that purpose.

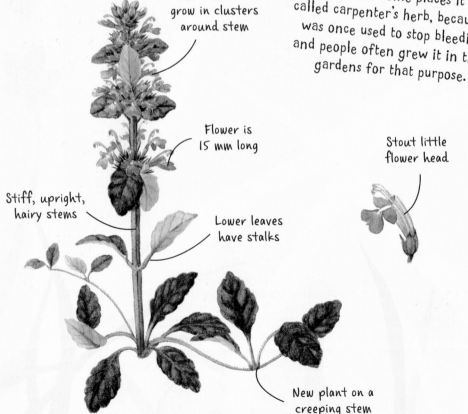

Small flowers
grow in clusters
around stem

Flower is
15 mm long

Stout little
flower head

Stiff, upright,
hairy stems

Lower leaves
have stalks

New plant on a
creeping stem

BUTTERWORT

These violet flowers attract bees, to pollinate them. A sticky leaf attracts flies and other small insects, holding them like glue and stopping them from breathing. The leaves then curl around the bugs and produce chemicals that start to dissolve their bodies. This releases nutrients that help the plant to grow.

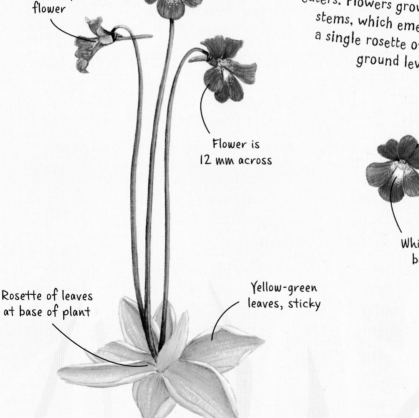

Funnel-shaped flower

Butterworts are pretty insect-eaters. Flowers grow from single stems, which emerge out of a single rosette of leaves at ground level.

Flower is 12 mm across

White at base

Rosette of leaves at base of plant

Yellow-green leaves, sticky

COLUMBINE

Columbine flowers grow on tall stems. The central part of the flower is made up of five petals, and a rosette of coloured leaves surrounds them, to create a drooping, stunning bloom. Wild columbines are deep blue to purple in colour and have a fragrance.

FACT FILE

Scientific name
Aquilegia vulgaris

Type Buttercup family

Size Up to 100 cm

Flowers May to August

Fruit Small and dry but with many seeds

Columbine is poisonous but it was once used to treat digestive problems, and as a painkiller. It was also thought that carrying a posy of columbine would make people fall in love.

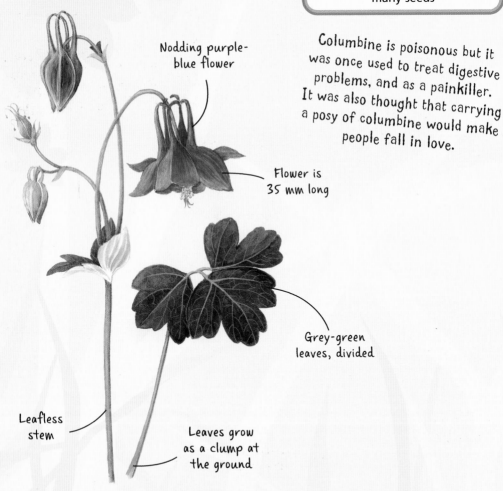

Nodding purple-blue flower

Flower is 35 mm long

Grey-green leaves, divided

Leafless stem

Leaves grow as a clump at the ground

CORNFLOWER

Cornflower blooms are such a brilliant blue that they have given their name to a shade of the colour. Each bloom is actually a collection of tiny flowers, called florets. The outer florets are blue to purple, and the inner florets are slightly redder. Cornflowers were once common in farmers' fields, but are now a rare sight.

FACT FILE

Scientific name
Centaurea cyanus

Type Daisy family

Size 40–90 cm

Flowers June to August

Fruit Small

Cornflowers were used in herbal medicine to treat eye problems, and young men in love often wore them in their buttonholes.

Inner floret

Tufted flower heads

Flower is 25 mm across

Outer floret

Stem is swollen just below the flower head

Narrow leaves, grey-green

Leaves grow alternately up the stem

DEVIL'S-BIT SCABIOUS

The round bloom of a Devil's-bit scabious is not one flower, but many little florets all clustered together. The petals are usually purple-blue, but are sometimes pinkish. The tiny anthers in each flower poke out above the petals. Bumblebees are drawn to the flowers because they prefer purple blooms to those of any other colour.

FACT FILE

Scientific name
Succisa pratensis

Type Teasel family

Size 10–75 cm

Flowers June to September

Fruit Dry and papery

This flower is rare, as each plant only produces a few heavy seeds that are not easily transported to new areas. It has also been killed off in many areas by the use of chemicals.

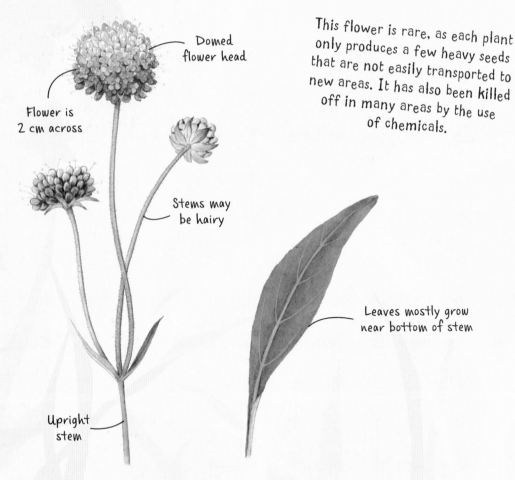

Domed flower head

Flower is 2 cm across

Stems may be hairy

Leaves mostly grow near bottom of stem

Upright stem

HAREBELL

The flowers of the harebell are delicate and swing when a breeze catches them. Each stem may bear just one flower, or several growing on a spike. The leaves grow long and thin near the flowers, but round when they are near the base. At ground level, creeping stems become thick and store food over winter for the plant.

FACT FILE

Scientific name
Campanula rotundifolia

Type Harebell family

Size 10–40 cm

Flowers July to October

Fruit Dry capsules

Harebells can live from year to year because they grow rhizomes. In the autumn, the plants die down but the rhizomes are safe in the ground, and produce new stems in the spring.

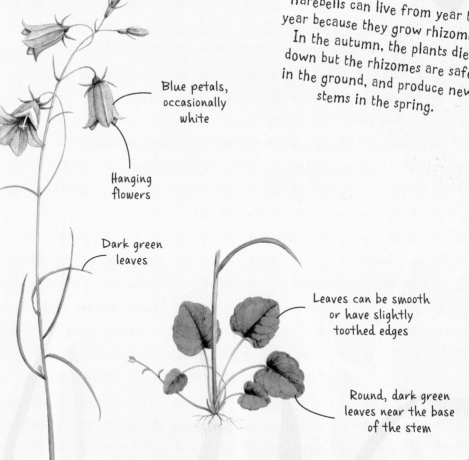

Blue petals, occasionally white

Hanging flowers

Dark green leaves

Leaves can be smooth or have slightly toothed edges

Round, dark green leaves near the base of the stem

MARSH VIOLET

Violets look like pansies, but are a
little smaller. Marsh violet flowers
are pale lilac or violet in colour and the
lower petal has deep purple veins. After
the flower dies the petals fall off, but
the five sepals stay attached to the stalk
and the growing seed capsule. The
caterpillars of fritillary butterflies use
this as a food plant.

FACT FILE

Scientific name
Viola palustris

Type Violet family

Size 5–20 cm

Flowers April to July

Fruit Egg-shaped

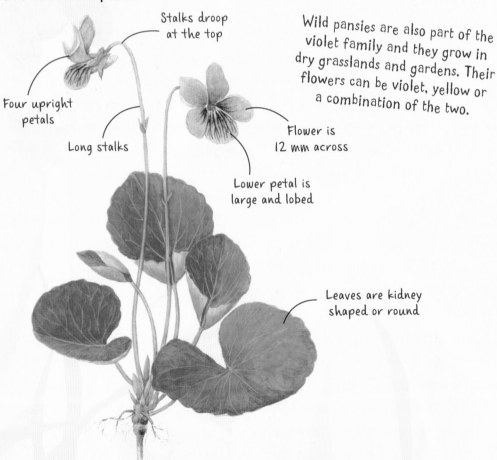

Stalks droop
at the top

Four upright
petals

Long stalks

Wild pansies are also part of the
violet family and they grow in
dry grasslands and gardens. Their
flowers can be violet, yellow or
a combination of the two.

Flower is
12 mm across

Lower petal is
large and lobed

Leaves are kidney
shaped or round

MEADOW CRANE'S BILL

The purple-blue flowers of the meadow crane's bill grow tall above the surface of a clump of dark green leaves, providing a summer splash of colour. These flowers grow all over Britain but look similar to wood crane's bill, which is paler in colour, but is only found in the north of England and Scotland.

Flowers grow in pairs

Flower is 3 cm across

Five petals

Fruit has a long 'beak'

Hairy stems

Large jagged leaves, round

Crane's bills are also called geraniums. They can survive from year to year, and grow in bigger and bigger mounds. Most geraniums are blue, violet, purple or pink.

TEASEL

Teasel plants produce flowers only in their second year. In the first year, the plant grows a large rosette of leaves at ground level. In the second year, a large stem grows from the rosette to hold the flower head. The rosette then dies back and paired prickly leaves grow on the flower stem.

FACT FILE

Scientific name
Dipascus fullonum

Type Teasel family

Size Up to 200 cm

Flowers July and August

Fruit Dry flower heads hold many dry fruits

Teasels are especially popular with goldfinches. These bold, noisy, colourful birds flock to the dry heads to feast on the seeds inside. A group of goldfinches is called a charm.

Flower is 7 cm long

Large flower head with purple flowers

Prickly leaves and flower stem

Leaves have no stalks and grow in pairs

TUFTED VETCH

Like other members of the pea family, tufted vetch has many oval leaflets that are paired on one stalk. Curling tendrils grow from the end of some leaflets. They help pea plants to climb and clamber high, catching the sun and blocking the light from other plants. The blue-purple flowers grow in clusters where leaflets connect to the stem.

FACT FILE

Scientific name
Vicia cracca

Type Pea family

Size 30–200 cm

Flowers June to August

Fruit Bright green pods

Clusters of flowers on a raceme

Tufted vetch is also known as cow vetch because it can be fed to cattle. It grows in wild woodlands where deer may roam. Like other pea plants, it adds goodness to the soil.

Up to 12 pairs of leaflets on one stalk; pairs are not exactly opposite

Long, hairy pods

Branched tendril

Blue-purple flower

Flower is 1 cm long

COWSLIP

Cowslips have rosettes of large, wrinkled leaves at the base and clusters of yellow flowers that are held high on tall stems. They were once widespread, but became less common in recent years. Today, hedgerows and meadows are often left uncut until autumn, so flowers like these have a better chance of surviving.

FACT FILE

Scientific name
Primula veris

Type Primrose family

Size 5–20 cm

Flowers April and May

Fruit Capsules

Cowslips have long been used in traditional medicine to treat coughs and headaches. They can also be made into wine, or used to add flavour and colour to recipes.

Yellow flowers in a cluster

Tall stem

Each leaf about 12 cm long

Tubular shaped sepals

Flower is 12 mm across

Thick, wrinkly leaves in a rosette

LESSER CELANDINE

Lesser celandine is a brief visitor to woodlands and other natural habitats. It grows as a patch of rosettes on the ground, topped by bright yellow flowers. However, it dies back once flowering has finished. The flowers contain between eight and 12 little petals, which only open when the sun is shining.

FACT FILE

Scientific name
Ranunculus ficaria

Type Buttercup family

Size 2–20 cm

Flowers March to May

Fruit Rounded seed heads

Lesser celandine is one of the first wildflowers to bloom. It provides food for insects, especially hungry bumblebees that have just come out of hibernation.

Eight petals around yellow stamens

Heart-shaped leaves

Flower is 2–3 cm across

Leaves are green and glossy

MARSH MARIGOLD

Marsh marigolds can form large clumps of deep green, shiny leaves, topped by bright golden flowers. The plants are tough and can survive in shady or sunny places, but they prefer damp soil. Marsh marigolds used to be common, but many of their marsh and bog habitats have been lost.

FACT FILE

Scientific name
Caltha palustris

Type Buttercup family

Size 20–30 cm

Flowers March to July

Fruit Capsules

These brightly coloured flowers were sometimes scattered over doorsteps in May. They were also used to remove warts and cure colds.

Flower is 25mm across

Five yellow sepals

Strong, upright stem

Kidney-shaped leaf

PRIMROSE

The yellow petals of the primrose are as pale as butter, but they turn orange near their bases. Primrose's Latin name – *Primula* – comes from the Latin for 'first little one' and 'primrose' means 'first rose'. This is one of the early spring flowering plants that bloom when there are few other flowers around.

FACT FILE

Scientific name
Primula vulgaris

Type Primrose family

Size 10–30 cm

Flowers March to June

Fruit Capsules

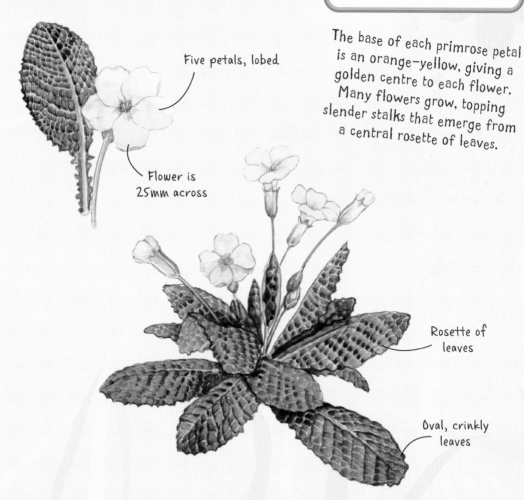

Five petals, lobed

Flower is 25mm across

The base of each primrose petal is an orange-yellow, giving a golden centre to each flower. Many flowers grow, topping slender stalks that emerge from a central rosette of leaves.

Rosette of leaves

Oval, crinkly leaves

DANDELION

One of the most common flowering plants, dandelions are found in gardens, parks and woodlands. They are considered weeds by many gardeners, but their bright-yellow flowers are a favourite of many pollinating insects. Other types of wildlife, such as rabbits, enjoy eating both flowers and leaves. The plants grow in a rosette shape, with the leaves and flower stem coming out of a central point, just above the tap root.

FACT FILE

Scientific name
Taraxacum officinale

Type Perennial weed

Size 5–74 cm

Flowers Yellow, from spring to autumn

Fruit Tiny seeds with fluffy hairs

Dandelions get their name from the old French name for the plant, dent de lion. This means 'tooth of the lion' because the leaf edges look like a row of sharp teeth.

Bright-yellow flowers

Dandelion seeds are fluffy and lightweight

Rosette of sepals (bud scales) around central stem

Long stalk

Hollow, fleshy flower stalk with white sap inside

Lobed leaves

SILVERWEED

This is a creeping plant that spreads out on bare soils. The feathery leaves are divided up into many pairs of leaflets that are covered in fine, silvery hairs. Long creeping stems, called stolons, grow on the ground beneath the leaves and flowers. Silverweed has been used in herbal remedies, and its roots were used to make tea.

FACT FILE

Scientific name
Potentilla anserina

Type Rose family

Size 5–20 cm

Flowers May to August

Fruit Dry and papery

Silverweed appears in many old stories and folklore. It was regarded as a useful plant, and its leaves were even put in shoes to keep feet dry!

Five petals

Silvery hairs on leaves

Flower is 15 mm across

Up to 12 leaflets on a leaf

Long, creeping stems have a red tint

YELLOW IRIS

Irises grow in wet places, and may even have their roots in water. They can spread by means of seeds, but also spread by rhizomes, which are swollen roots that produce buds in spring. When they spread by rhizomes, irises can quickly grow into large clumps and create a perfect habitat for pond wildlife.

FACT FILE

Scientific name
Iris pseudocorus

Type Grow from rhizomes

Size Up to 100 cm

Flowers June to August

Fruit Three-sided and long

Long, slender anthers

Flower is 9 cm across

Large green sepals protect flower bud

Ducks, fish and insects can hide among iris plants. Yellow irises remove dirt from water, and are used in sewage farms.

Large flowers with floppy petals

Long, slender leaves may survive mild winters

YELLOW RATTLE

Yellow rattle steals nutrients from its neighbouring plants. It stops grass from growing, which helps other types of wild plant to survive in meadows. At the end of the summer the seed capsules ripen and seeds inside become loose. When the capsule is shaken, the seeds rattle around, which is how the plant got its name.

FACT FILE

Scientific name
Rhinanthus minor

Type Figwort family

Size 20–40 cm

Flowers June to September

Fruit Dry capsules with seeds that rattle

The stems of yellow rattle have unusual black marks on them, which helps to identify this meadow wildflower. The yellow flowers are small, and protected by green bracts.

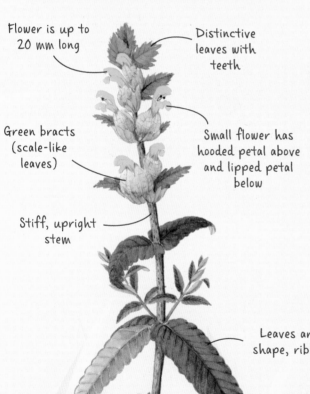

Flower is up to 20 mm long

Distinctive leaves with teeth

Green bracts (scale-like leaves)

Small flower has hooded petal above and lipped petal below

Stiff, upright stem

Leaves are triangular in shape, ribbed and toothed

ALDER

The wood of the alder is fascinating – when it is submerged in water, it becomes as hard as stone. Much of the Italian city of Venice is built on piles of alder wood, which were sunk into the sand banks. Houses and other buildings were then built on top. The small, winged seeds of this water-loving tree get carried along by streams and rivers to grow further downstream.

FACT FILE

Scientific name
Populus tremula

Height 18–25 m

Where Widespread; woodland, hedgerows, often near water

Flowering February/March

Fruiting October–December

It is said that the green dye of the alder flower was used to colour the clothes of Robin Hood.

Rounded with toothed edges

Smaller female catkins develop into cones (fruit)

Male catkins (flowers) are up to 5 cm long

Side buds are on short stalks

Mature cones are woody and open to release seeds

Shiny and dark green in colour

APPLE

Popular in many gardens throughout northern Europe, apple trees provide plenty of food and shelter for wildlife, including bugs and birds. Their tasty fruits can be eaten straight from the tree by humans, pressed to make juice and cider, or cooked to make sauces and puddings. There are many different varieties, or types, of apple tree. Bramley apples are larger than other varieties and are too sour to eat raw.

FACT FILE

Scientific name *Malus pumila*
Height 6–10 m
Where Woodland, orchards
Flowering April–June
Fruiting June–August

Apples were probably one of the first fruits to be grown for food, and they have been an important source of food in cooler countries for thousands of years.

Large, rounded crown

Bud

Tree shape after losing its leaves

Pale-pink flowers in small clusters

Finely toothed leaves

Large green and red fruits

ASPEN

Fluttering leaves, which tremble in the breeze, give the aspen its Latin name, *tremula*, and its common name of 'quaking aspen'. The autumn-dry leaves of the aspen produce a rustling noise even in gentle breezes. In Medieval times, the timber was used to make houses for the poor who could not afford oak.

Herbalists once used its flowers to treat people suffering from anxiety or nightmares.

Male and female catkins (flowers) grow on separate trees

Male catkins are reddish purple and up to 8 cm long

Buds have pointed tips

Green female catkins develop into seed capsules (fruit) that contain many hairy seeds

In summer, new leaves emerge coppery brown, turning to green

Rounded or slightly oval

Tiny, fluffy seeds are easily carried in the wind

BEECH

Beech trees have long been part of Britain's history, especially in the furniture-making industry. Particularly grand trees have been called 'queen beeches', and impressive beech woods are known as 'nature's cathedrals'. Since Roman times, beech wood was used for fuel. Its nuts – called mast – were used as feed for animals.

FACT FILE

Scientific name *Fagus sylvatica*

Height 10–35 m

Where Woodland, chalky or sandy soils

Flowering April/May

Fruiting September–November

Beech was the preferred wood for making furniture due to its pink-orange colouring.

Long, narrow buds

Male flowers hang on long stems

Female flowers are green and spiky on short stems

Pointed tip

One or two nuts are held in a prickly four-lobed casing (fruit)

Triangular, shiny, brown nuts are called mast

Glossy and dark green

BLACK POPLAR

Once common along riverbanks, today the native black poplar is very rare and found only in southern England and parts of Ireland. Only a few hundred female black poplar trees exist in Britain and few of them grow near males. This means that seeds are rarely produced, so new trees are hard to find.

FACT FILE

Scientific name *Populus nigra*

Height 20–25 m

Where Southern England; near water

Flowering March/April

Fruiting April/May

Arrows found on the wreck of the Mary Rose were made of black poplar wood — they had survived 400 years under the sea.

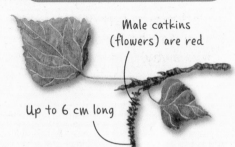

Male catkins (flowers) are red

Up to 6 cm long

Green female catkins develop into seed capsules (fruit)

Fine tooth on edge

Seed capsules contain brown, cottony seeds

Smooth and tan coloured

Can range from diamond to triangular in shape

BLACKTHORN

This deciduous tree is distinctive because its flowers are some of the first to appear in spring, appearing even before its leaves. The fruits of the blackthorn are known as sloes and, although bitter to taste, they are popular with birds. It has long been considered a magical tree. In Celtic mythology it was home to fairies, and a blackthorn staff (long stick) was thought to be ideal for keeping evil spirits away.

FACT FILE

Scientific name *Prunus spinosa*

Height 6–7 m

Where Widespread; woodland, scrubland, hedgerows

Flowering March/April

Fruiting August/September

Sharply pointed, stiff spines

Fruits are blue-black berries, called sloes

Dark, almost black in colour, and spiny

Tiny, white, scented flowers have five petals and emerge before the leaves

Dull green, 2–4 cm long

Finely toothed edge

BUCKTHORN

In the past, plants and trees were used to treat illnesses and buckthorn is no exception. The ripe, black berries are mildly poisonous to humans, but they are a source of food for many birds. When herbal remedies were common, a tea made from buckthorn berries was used to treat a stomach ache, even though it causes vomiting and diarrhoea! The bark of a young tree is orange-brown and darkens with age.

FACT FILE

Scientific name
Rhamnus cathartica

Height 4–6 m

Where Widespread; hedgerows, woodland

Flowering May/June

Fruiting September/October

Small, yellow, four-petalled flowers are scented

Flowers grow in clusters

Sharp thorn at tip

Fruits are berries that contain two to four seeds each

Pointed tip

Shiny, black berries are up to 8 mm long

Dark and glossy with a smooth surface

COMMON LIME

The widely planted common lime is easy to spot as its leaves, and anything under them, get covered in a sticky substance called honeydew. Tiny insects called aphids suck sap (a sugary liquid) from the tree and produce honeydew. This attracts dirt, and by autumn, the leaves are sticky and filthy and so are cars that may be parked beneath its branches.

Beekeepers often place their hives near lime trees so that the bees produce 'lime honey'.

Red buds

5–10 cm long with a pointed tip

Groups of small, scented, yellow, five-petalled flowers hang on long stalks

An extra leaflet, called a bract, helps the fruits to travel in the wind

Slightly heart-shaped with tufts of hair on the underside

Look at the back of the leaf — if it has small clumps of red hairs at the base of the veins, it could be a small-leaved lime

Small, hard, round fruits

Oval • TREES & SHRUBS (327)

DOGWOOD

This small tree or shrub has red stems that are especially noticeable in winter when there are few colours to brighten the dark days. Dogwood has nothing to do with dogs. The wood is hard and was once used to make skewers known as 'dags'. This gave the tree its old name of dagswood. The leaves of dogwood can be identified by gently pulling them apart – stringy latex can be seen where the veins have been broken.

FACT FILE

Scientific name
Cornus sanguinea

Height 2–5 m

Where Widespread; woodland, scrubland, hedgerows

Flowering May/June

Fruiting September–November

Small, white, bad-smelling flowers grow in clusters

Flowers have four petals and are up to 1 cm across

Smooth edges and deep veins with a pointed tip

Reddish in colour

Fruits are black, pea-sized berries

Berries are bitter to taste and not good to eat

Leaves turn dark red in autumn

ENGLISH ELM

English elms were common in Britain, until the onset of Dutch elm disease killed 25 million of them in the 1970s. It is thought that this tree was introduced to Britain 2000 years ago by the Romans, and some scientific research suggests that all English elms descended from just one tree. This meant that many elms were equally vulnerable to disease. Today, elms can often be seen growing in hedgerows.

FACT FILE

Scientific name *Ulmus procera*

Height 16–30 m

Where Widespread; woodland, hedgerows

Flowering February/March

Fruiting April–June

Fruits are on short stalks

Papery, winged fruits contain one seed each

Thick and reddish in colour

Purple flowers are in small clusters

Flowers appear before the leaves

Toothed edges

One side is longer than the other, similar to the wych elm

GOAT WILLOW

The goat willow is also known as 'pussy willow' because its springtime male catkins are soft and grey – like a cat's paw. Goat willows are important trees in woodland and hedgerows because they are linked with many types of butterfly and moth. Some larvae feed on the leaves and others live under the bark. As the male catkins mature and turn yellow they are called 'goslings' because they are the same colour as baby geese.

FACT FILE

Scientific name
Salix caprea

Height 4–10 m

Where Widespread; woodland, hedgerows

Flowering May

Fruiting October/November

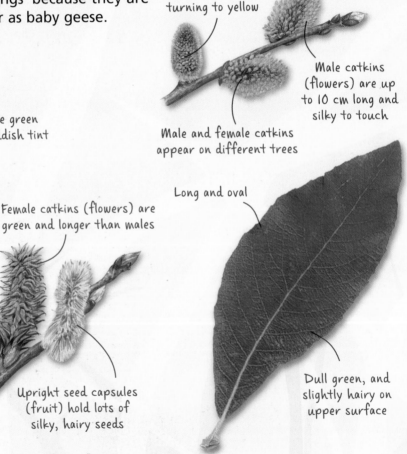

Grey at first, turning to yellow

Male catkins (flowers) are up to 10 cm long and silky to touch

Male and female catkins appear on different trees

Buds are green with a reddish tint

Long and oval

Female catkins (flowers) are green and longer than males

Upright seed capsules (fruit) hold lots of silky, hairy seeds

Dull green, and slightly hairy on upper surface

HAZEL

As hazel catkins turn yellow it's a sign that spring is coming, and when squirrels start to gather hazelnuts winter is just around the corner. Hazels are not only a source of food for many types of wildlife, but they provide home and shelter for them, too. They often grow in dense clusters with lots of stems growing from the ground, rather than a single trunk.

FACT FILE

Scientific name *Corylus avellana*

Height 12–15 m

Where Widespread; woodland, scrubland, hedgerows

Flowering February

Fruiting August/September

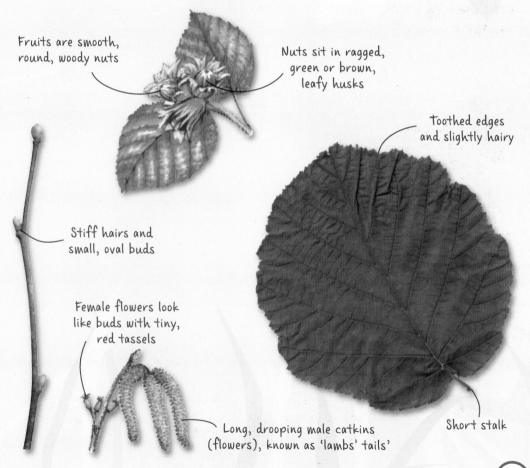

Fruits are smooth, round, woody nuts

Nuts sit in ragged, green or brown, leafy husks

Toothed edges and slightly hairy

Stiff hairs and small, oval buds

Female flowers look like buds with tiny, red tassels

Long, drooping male catkins (flowers), known as 'lambs' tails'

Short stalk

Oval • TREES & SHRUBS (331)

HORNBEAM

The statuesque hornbeam is an impressive deciduous tree with its pale silvery-grey bark, and yellow-green catkins in the spring. It's often coppiced (stems cut back to the ground causing many long shoots to grow) or pollarded (top branches cut) and it is commonly planted for hedging. The white wood is very fine-grained, which makes particularly good firewood and charcoal.

FACT FILE

Scientific name
Carpinus betulus

Height 10–20 m

Where Southern and eastern England; woodland, hedgerows

Flowering March

Fruiting September

The Romans made their chariots from hornbeam wood because of its strength.

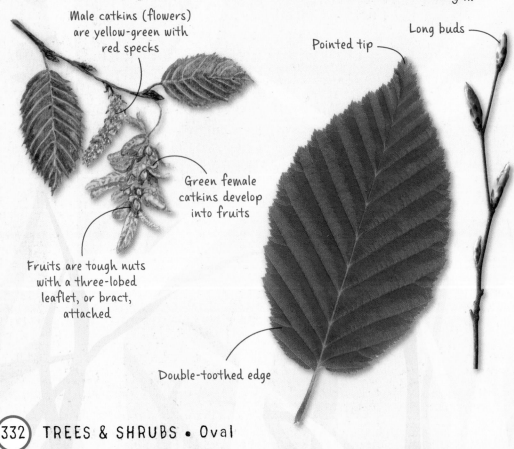

Male catkins (flowers) are yellow-green with red specks

Green female catkins develop into fruits

Fruits are tough nuts with a three-lobed leaflet, or bract, attached

Pointed tip

Long buds

Double-toothed edge

MULBERRY

The black mulberry tree has a long history rooted in Southeast Asia where it has been cultivated for thousands of years. It was introduced to Europe by the Romans, who dedicated the tree to Minerva, goddess of Wisdom. It has been widely planted and is grown in sheltered gardens for its delicious fruits, which contain a staining dye.

Mulberry is celebrated in the nursery rhyme, 'Here we go round the mulberry bush'.

Green female flowers are 1–2 cm long

Male flowers are yellow-green and longer than the female flowers

Fruits are sweet when ripe

Rough to touch on upper side

Buds are broad and pointed

Raspberry-like fruits are purple-red when ripe

Toothed edges

PEAR

The pear tree originally came from Southwest Asia, but is now common throughout Europe. Pears have undergone many changes since they first arrived in Europe as farmers have cultivated sweeter and juicier varieties of the fruit. Pear trees can be found in gardens and orchards in Britain, especially southern areas. The wild pear, which is a different type, is rare, and its fruits are hard, gritty and smaller than those of the *Pyrus communis*.

FACT FILE

Scientific name *Pyrus communis*

Height 9–15 m

Where Southern England; orchards, woodland, gardens

Flowering March/April

Fruiting September/October

Centres are pink-purple

Reddish-brown and hairy when young

Flowers have five pure-white petals

Pears ripen to yellow-green, sometimes slightly rosy

Pointed tip

Fruits are hard pears up to 12 cm long

Smooth or finely toothed edge, up to 8 cm long

PLUM

Plum trees are most commonly found growing in orchards and gardens. Plums were probably created as a hybrid (mix) of blackthorn and cherry plum. Today, plums are the second most cultivated fruit in the world. The plum *Prunus domestica* is first mentioned in 479 BC in the writings of the Chinese philosopher Confucius – it is listed as a popular food in Chinese culture. A tree will not produce fruit until it is four or five years old.

Clusters of flowers

Flowers are all-white, sometimes tinged with green

Smooth and brown

Smooth skin

Purple fruits are large, round and juicy

Finely toothed edges

Upper surface is smooth and lower surface has tiny hairs

Oval • TREES & SHRUBS

SILVER BIRCH

With its silvery bark and fluttering leaves, the silver birch is sometimes called 'Queen of the forest'. It was one of the first trees to start growing in Britain at the end of the Ice Age, around 10,000 years ago. Silver birch is known as a pioneer species, which means it is one of the first plants to grow in a new area. Silver birch produces huge crops of seeds of up to one million every year. This tree is easily recognizable by its silver-grey bark, even in winter.

FACT FILE

Scientific name *Betula pendula*

Height 18–25 m

Where Widespread; woodland, scrubland

Flowering April–May

Fruiting June

Winged seeds are 1 to 2 mm long and are released from the fruits

Brown, with small bumps, or warts

Slender, green female catkins (flowers) develop into seed capsules (fruit)

Male catkins are long, drooping and yellow

Double-toothed edges

WAYFARING TREE

Once common alongside footpaths in southern England, the wayfaring tree grows in hedgerows, scrubland or on chalky ground. Today, it is a more common sight in gardens, grown for its ornamental leaves, large flower heads and bright berries. Despite their attractive appearance, the berries are mildly poisonous and should not be eaten. The young, flexible stems can be used to make twine.

FACT FILE

Scientific name
Viburnum lantana

Height Up to 6 m

Where South England and Wales; hedgerows, scrubland,

Flowering May

Fruiting August/September

Flowers have five petals

White flowers appear in dense clusters

Underside is hairy

Rough upper surface with deep veins

Grey-brown and hairy

Fruits are oval berries that turn black when ripe

Berries are up to 8 mm long

WHITEBEAM

When the leaves of the whitebeam first open in the spring they appear white, giving this tree its name ('beam' is the Saxon word for tree). The whiteness is caused by the young leaves' soft coating of white hairs. Hair on the topside soon disappears as the leaves mature and droop downwards, but the undersides stay white. The wood of the whitebeam is very hard-wearing.

FACT FILE

Scientific name *Sorbus aria*

Height 8–15 m

Where Southern England; woodland, chalky soils

Flowering May/June

Fruiting September

The small, red fruits of the whitebeam can be made into jam and wine.

Green buds

White hairs on the underside

White flowers grow in loose clusters

Each berry contains two seeds

Fruits are oval-shaped berries that turn red when ripe

Up to 8 cm long

TREES & SHRUBS • Oval

WILD CHERRY

When its branches are laden with white flowers or bunches of glossy fruits, the wild cherry attracts many birds. According to folklore, this tree has particular associations with cuckoos. The birds are believed to need three good meals of cherries before they will stop singing. The wood of a cherry tree is fine-grained and a beautiful shade of red, making it popular with cabinet makers.

FACT FILE

Scientific name *Prunus avium*

Height 18–25 m

Where Widespread; parks, woodland

Flowering April/May

Fruiting July/August

White, five-petalled flowers grow in groups of up to six

Long, pointed tip

Berry-like fruits ripen to red

Brownish red buds

Up to 15 cm long with toothed edges

WILD PRIVET

For centuries, gardeners have taken wild trees and shrubs, such as privet, and grown them as ornamental plants. Privet is one of a few trees and shrubs that is described as being semi-evergreen. Depending on climate, it may or may not lose its leaves in winter. Privet is commonly grown in gardens, cut neatly into hedges, but the wild form looks very different, with long branches that reach upwards.

The flowers and fruits were once used to treat eye and mouth diseases despite being poisonous.

Flowers grow in cone-shaped clusters

Cream-coloured, sweet-scented flowers attract insects

Flowers develop into fruits

Fruits are shiny, black berries

Small and shiny

Young twigs are covered in short hairs

WYCH ELM

In Middle English (a language spoken long ago) the word 'wych' meant bendy. Wych elm trees are not particularly bendy, but their young shoots are and they can be bent and twisted for making into baskets and other goods. These trees were badly affected by Dutch elm disease – a fungus carried by a wood-boring beetle.

FACT FILE

Scientific name *Ulmus glabra*

Height 16–30 m

Where Widespread; hedgerows, woodland

Flowering February/March

Fruiting May/June

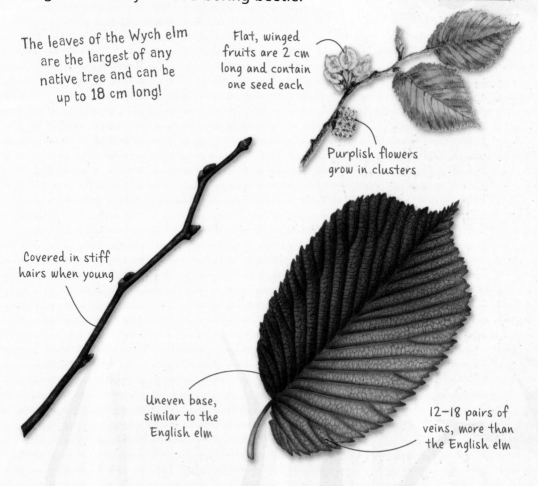

The leaves of the Wych elm are the largest of any native tree and can be up to 18 cm long!

Flat, winged fruits are 2 cm long and contain one seed each

Purplish flowers grow in clusters

Covered in stiff hairs when young

Uneven base, similar to the English elm

12–18 pairs of veins, more than the English elm

BUDDLEIA

Often known as a butterfly bush, buddleia can grow as tall as some trees, reaching more than 4 m in height. It is a popular garden plant because it has attractive flowers with a strong scent, and is visited regularly by butterflies. The woody stems arch high, and have unusually shaped flower heads, called panicles. A panicle is actually made up of lots of tiny flowers, each with four small petals.

The butterfly bush got its Latin name, buddleia, from Reverend Adam Buddle (1660–1715) who was a keen collector of plants.

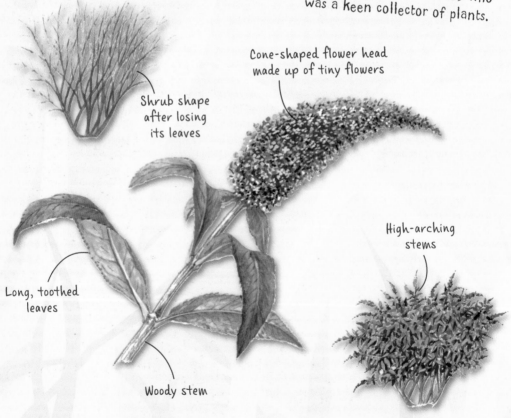

Shrub shape after losing its leaves

Cone-shaped flower head made up of tiny flowers

High-arching stems

Long, toothed leaves

Woody stem

MAGNOLIA

With their enormous, fragrant blooms and clusters of red seeds, **magnolias are impressive trees.** They originally came from the United States and are the state flowers of Mississippi and Louisiana. Magnolias are normally fertilized by beetles. Its petals are unusually tough, which minimises damage by the crawling insects.

FACT FILE

Scientific name
Magnolia grandiflora
Height 12–25 m
Where Widespread; gardens, parks, arboretums
Flowering June–August
Fruiting September–December

Magnolia is named after Pierre Magnol (1638–1715), a French botanist, and many different varieties have been cultivated.

Furry seed capsules (fruit) are up to 6 cm long and turn from green to orange-pink

Seed capsules open to release red seeds

Thick and glossy with smooth edges

Six to 12 petals

Large, white, scented flowers up to 25 cm across

Up to 16 cm long

HOLLY

Throughout the cold winter months, holly is one of the few plants that provide colour. The deep-green leaves remain glossy and vibrant when so much else has died down, and bright-red holly berries attract winter birds to the garden. Holly can grow as a small, regularly pruned bush, or it can be allowed to grow into a tree reaching up to 10 m in height. Holly berries are poisonous to humans.

FACT FILE

Scientific name *Ilex aquifolium*
Height 8–10 m
Where Woodland, hedgerows, scrubland
Flowering Small and white, from late spring to summer
Fruiting Red berries, from autumn to winter

Holly berries are used as a Christmas decoration, particularly in wreaths. However, in cold weather, birds often strip the trees and bushes long before December.

White, scented male flowers grow in tight clusters on separate trees

Flowers have four petals

White female flowers grow near the base of leaves on female trees

Sharp, pointed edges

Female flowers develop into shiny, red berries

Dark and glossy

PEDUNCULATE OAK

The pedunculate, or English, oak is known as the 'King of the forest' and it has a rich history, featuring in many myths and legends. English oaks provide a unique habitat for hundreds of species of other plants and animals. Oaks attract insects, which in turn attract birds, and acorns provide food for squirrels and other small mammals.

FACT FILE

Scientific name *Quercus robur*

Height 15–25 m

Where Widespread; ancient woodland

Flowering May

Fruiting October

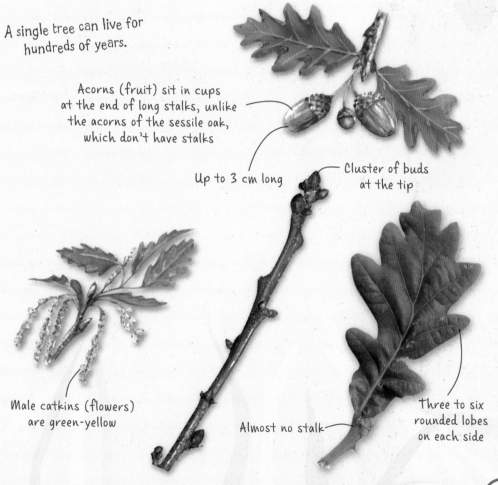

A single tree can live for hundreds of years.

Acorns (fruit) sit in cups at the end of long stalks, unlike the acorns of the sessile oak, which don't have stalks

Up to 3 cm long

Cluster of buds at the tip

Male catkins (flowers) are green-yellow

Almost no stalk

Three to six rounded lobes on each side

SEA BUCKTHORN

This small deciduous shrub can be found growing on exposed, windy coastlines in salty conditions that few other trees can tolerate. Sea buckthorn is an increasingly popular plant that is cultivated for the extraordinary properties of its bright-orange berries and its deep and widespread roots. Its roots help to bind loose soil and add nitrogen to it, which is important for soil fertility.

FACT FILE

Scientific name
Hippophae rhamnoides

Height 1–3 m

Where Widespread; coastal areas, sand dunes

Flowering March/April

Fruiting September

The berries are full of vitamin C and are used in skincare products.

Male flowers are up to 4 mm across and grow on separate trees to the females

Green male flowers have leaf-like petals

Fruits are bright-orange berries that grow on the female trees

Up to 8 mm long

Up to 6 cm long and 1 cm wide

Silvery-green, long and slender

Thorny, and develops silvery scales

SESSILE OAK

The sessile oak is one of just two native British oaks, but there are hundreds of different types in the northern hemisphere alone. The sessile oak is more likely to be found in stony uplands than the pedunculate oak, but they are similar in appearance. In Anglo-Saxon times, an oak was called an 'aik' and a seed was an 'aik-com', hence today's name – acorn.

In one year, a mature oak tree produces as many as 50,000 acorns.

Paler underneath with hairs on veins

Orange-brown buds

Male catkins are yellow and drooping

Hard-shelled acorns (fruit) grow in clusters

Sessile acorns do not have stalks, unlike pedunculate acorns which have long stalks

Leaf stalks are 1–2 cm – much longer than those of the pedunculate oak

SPINDLE

Spindles more often resemble bushes than trees, and they are often seen in hedgerows and woodlands. The timber of this plant was once used to make spindles – round, spinning pieces of wood that wool is wound onto. This gave the spindle tree its common name. The poisonous berries contain orange seeds that can be boiled to make a yellow dye.

The berries have been used in traditional remedies to cure farm animals of skin complaints.

Flowers grow in loose clusters

Green with shoots coming off at many angles

Flowers have four green-white petals

Each seed pod (fruit) is divided into four parts

Long and oval-shaped with finely toothed edges

Red seed pods open to release four small, orange seeds

Leaves turn orange and red in autumn

SWEET CHESTNUT

These trees produce large, edible nuts that can be roasted and are often sold in streets, at fairs and other winter events. Sweet chestnuts are native to the warmer parts of Europe and were first brought to Britain by Roman soldiers, who relied on the nuts as an important part of their diet. Sweet chestnuts do not always ripen fully in Britain.

FACT FILE

Scientific name *Castanea sativa*

Height 20–30 m

Where Widespread; woodland, parks, well-drained soil

Flowering June/July

Fruiting October/November

Sweet chestnuts have been long associated with winter festivals and were once seen as sources of magic.

Fruits open to reveal one to three glossy, brown nuts

Spiky, green casing

Long, male catkins (flowers) can grow as long as the leaves

Sharply toothed edges

Green, spiky female flowers grow at the base of the catkin

Tiny white dots, or warts, along twig

10–25 cm long

WHITE WILLOW

The white willow grows well in damp soil and so is most likely to be found alongside streams and ponds, often near alder trees. Animals, especially horses, enjoy nibbling the leaves and tender shoots of this tree. The pale brown wood of the white willow burns easily and quickly. This tree can be pollarded every four or five years to produce a crop of straight poles, which are used for making fences.

FACT FILE

Scientific name *Salix alba*

Height 20–25 m

Where Widespread; often near water

Flowering April/May

Fruiting June–August

Female catkins (flowers) are green and appear on separate trees to the males

Female catkins develop into seed capsules, full of hairy seeds

Finely toothed edges

Grey to pale brown in colour

Golden yellow with fine hairs

Male catkins are yellow

Long and narrow

FIELD MAPLE

The field maple provides an ideal habitat for many small creatures, and plants such as lichens and mosses. Field maples are often found growing in hedgerows. In autumn, they can be identified by their leaves, which turn red and yellow. According to ancient myths, a child could be guaranteed a long life by being passed through the branches of a field maple.

FACT FILE

Scientific name *Acer campestre*

Height 8–14 m

Where Widespread; woodland, hedgerows

Flowering April

Fruiting June/July

In some places, it was thought that field maples could protect a house against bats.

White-green flowers have five petals

The wings are in a straight line, not curved as in the sycamore

4–7 cm long, smaller than a sycamore

Three to five rounded lobes

Brown and coated in soft hairs

Hand-shaped • TREES & SHRUBS

GUELDER ROSE

Despite its name, this shrub is not a rose at all, but more closely related to the elder. Its unusual name comes from the Dutch province of Guelderland where it was grown as a decorative garden plant. Guelder rose berries are popular with birds, such as bullfinches, and small animals, but they are poisonous to humans.

FACT FILE

Scientific name
Viburnum opulus
Height Up to 4 m
Where Woodland, scrubland, hedgerows, damp soil
Flowering June/July
Fruiting September

The berries of the guelder rose can be used to make a red ink.

Poisonous berries contain one seed each

Central flowers develop into red berries (fruit)

Buds grow in opposite pairs

Clusters of small, white flowers are encircled by larger flowers

8 cm long with three large lobes

Scented flowers have five petals

Leaves turn reddish-brown in autumn

HAWTHORN

The hawthorn's leaves appear quickly in spring and its white blossom is a sign that summer is on its way. In folklore, in North Wales, hawthorn was associated with death, possibly because the flowers' scent reminds some people of rotting flesh. However, the berries, leaves and flowers have been used in many past medicines. It also has long associations with May Day – its wood was used to make the first Maypoles.

FACT FILE

Scientific name
Crataegus monogyna

Height 12–15 m

Where Widespread; hedgerows, scrubland

Flowering May/June

Fruiting March/April

Hawthorn was once believed to provide protection againsy vampires by forming a magical barrier.

Long thorns up to 1.5 cm long

Dark green

Small, white, scented flowers grow in clusters after the leaves have appeared

Stiff with brown buds

Deep red, oval-shaped fruits called haws

Haws contain one seed each, unlike those of the Midland hawthorn, which contain two

Three to seven deep lobes

Hand-shaped • TREES & SHRUBS (353)

HORSE CHESTNUT

Horse chestnuts are best known for their glossy, brown nuts known as conkers. Competitors meet up in Northamptonshire every year to battle in the World Conker Championships – an event that has been running since 1965. Horse chestnut trees arrived in Britain in the 16th century and possibly get their name from the practice of feeding conkers to horses to cure them of illness.

FACT FILE

Scientific name
Aesculus hippocastanum
Height 14–28 m
Where Widespread; woodland, parks, hedgerows
Flowering May
Fruiting September/October

Upright spikes of white flowers

Flowers have five petals and a small pink spot near the centre

One brown nut, or conker, inside each spiky, green fruit

Sticky buds

Leaves are made up of five to seven long leaflets and appear in early spring

Leaflets fan out and are on a sturdy stalk

LONDON PLANE

London plane trees are a familiar sight in many cities and towns. They were widely planted along streets in urban areas because they tolerate pollution. In the 17th century, American plane and oriental plane trees were cross-bred to produce this new variety. The London plane sheds dirt in its bark, which peels off through the year revealing a paler yellow bark beneath. Its attractive, hard-wearing timber is also known as 'lacewood'.

FACT FILE

Scientific name
Platanus x hispanica

Height 13–35 m

Where Widespread; streets, parks, cities, towns

Flowering May/June

Fruiting September/October

Each spiky fruit contains many seeds

Male flowers are round and yellow

Lobes have triangular tips

Female flowers are round and reddish

Many fruit cases stay on the tree throughout the winter

Up to 25 cm long

Green with smooth, pink buds

Hand-shaped • TREES & SHRUBS

SYCAMORE

In the autumn, sycamores produce thousands of spinning, winged fruits called 'keys'. The wings act like helicopter blades and spin the keys through the air so that they land some distance from the tree. The sycamore is also known as the martyrs' tree. In England in 1834, a group of workers – the Tolpuddle Martyrs – met under a sycamore to form a society to fight for better wages. They were expelled from the country as punishment.

FACT FILE

Scientific name
Acer pseudoplatanus

Height 16–35 m

Where Woodland, hedgerows, mountains

Flowering April/May

Fruiting September

Green buds grow in opposite pairs

Each key holds two seeds

Each individual flower has five petals

Yellow-green flowers hang in spikes

Winged fruits, or keys, are green at first, then ripen to brown

Up to 15 cm long with five lobes

Stalks are often red

WILD SERVICE TREE

The wild service tree is an indicator of ancient woodland – areas where there has been continuous woodland since at least 1600. In spring, white blossom covers this tree and in autumn, its leaves turn coppery-red. Its berries, which were used to cure stomach upsets until the 1700s, are best eaten when overripe. This tree also goes by the name of 'chequers'. Some say this refers to the bark peeling off in squares and leaving a chequerboard effect.

FACT FILE

Scientific name
Sorbus torminalis

Height 10–25 m

Where Southern England, Wales; ancient woodland

Flowering May/June

Fruiting September–November

Stalks are hairy

Reddish-brown, berry-like fruits

Small white flowers hang in clusters on stalks

Slightly glossy on upper surface

Green buds

Up to 10 cm long

ASH

The stately ash is one of the tallest deciduous trees in Europe and it grows easily in many habitats across Britain. In Scandinavian mythology, the ash was regarded as the tree of life. In English folklore, it was used to predict the weather. If oak buds opened before ash buds then the summer would be dry, but if ash buds opened first, the summer would be wet.

FACT FILE

Scientific name
Fraxinus excelsior
Height 15–30 m
Where Widespread; woodland, hedgerows, hillsides
Flowering April
Fruiting June

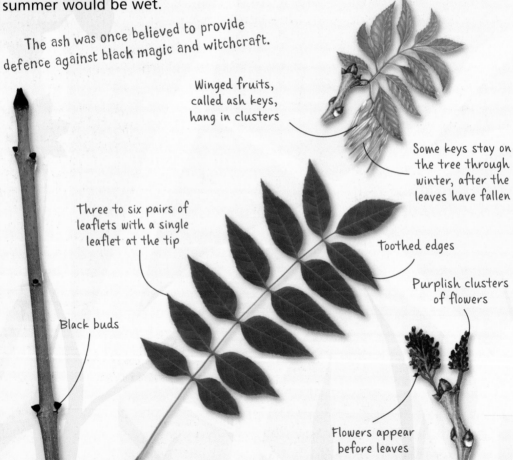

The ash was once believed to provide defence against black magic and witchcraft.

Winged fruits, called ash keys, hang in clusters

Some keys stay on the tree through winter, after the leaves have fallen

Three to six pairs of leaflets with a single leaflet at the tip

Toothed edges

Purplish clusters of flowers

Black buds

Flowers appear before leaves

BRAMBLE

Also known as blackberry bushes, brambles have prickly, woody stems that can grow up to 3 m in length. Each stem can grow up or out, arching over other plants. Sometimes, the stems reach the ground where they will then grow roots. The flowers are pink or white, and appear in late spring or early summer. Bramble shrubs often grow up fences or walls, where they are protected from winds and bathed in sunshine, which ripens the fruits.

FACT FILE

Scientific name
Rubus fruticosus
Height Up to 3 m
Where Gardens, hedgerows
Flowering May–September
Fruiting July–November

Bramble is closely related to the rose – it has sharp, curved thorns along its stem to deter animals from eating the fruits.

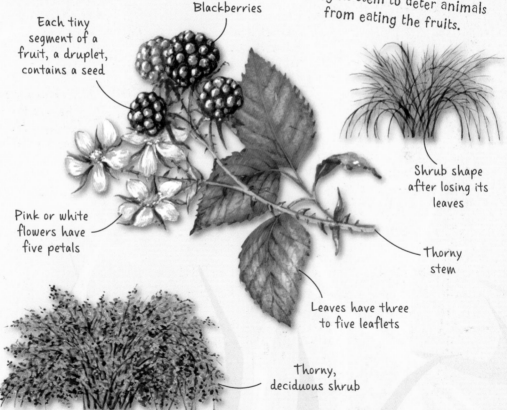

Each tiny segment of a fruit, a druplet, contains a seed

Blackberries

Shrub shape after losing its leaves

Pink or white flowers have five petals

Thorny stem

Leaves have three to five leaflets

Thorny, deciduous shrub

DOG ROSE

Roses are flowering shrubs that have been traditional garden plants for centuries, particularly in cooler climates where they thrive. Wild types, called dog roses, are most often found in hedgerows or growing along fences where they attract many insects and birds. Garden roses are normally grown for their beautiful flowers, variety of colours and strong scent. The stems are usually thorny, and the red fruits, called hips, appear in autumn.

Rose hips have unusual names, such as pixie pears and pigs' noses. They can be used to make teas, rich in vitamin C, by boiling them for at least ten minutes.

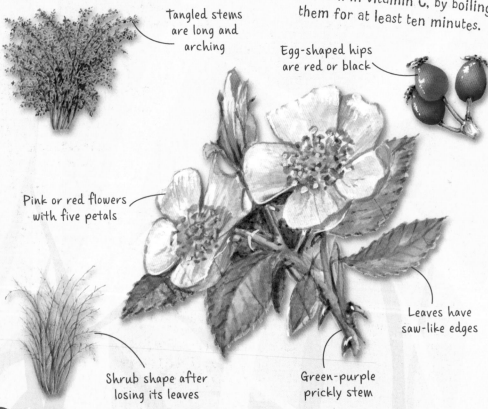

Tangled stems are long and arching

Egg-shaped hips are red or black

Pink or red flowers with five petals

Leaves have saw-like edges

Shrub shape after losing its leaves

Green-purple prickly stem

ELDER

The elder has proved to be a useful British tree, with the flowers, berries and stems all being put to good use. 'Elder' comes from the Anglo Saxon word *aeld* meaning 'fire'. The stems are hollow and were once used to blow air into fires. In Denmark, the tree was associated with magic and, before a tree could be cut down, permission had to be sought from its spirit.

FACT FILE

Scientific name *Sambucus nigra*
Height Up to 10 m
Where Widespread; hedgerows, scrubland
Flowering June/July
Fruiting August/September

The flowers can be made into a cordial and the berries into wine.

Small, shiny, black berries (fruit) on red stalks

Heavy clusters hang downwards

Each tiny flower has three to five petals

Each leaflet is oval in shape

Soft and white in centre

Pale flowers have a sickly fragrance

Each stalk has two to four pairs of small leaflets with a single one at the tip

Compound • TREES & SHRUBS

LABURNUM

A common sight in British gardens, laburnum is recognizable by its cascades of bright-yellow flowers in the summer. It originated in Europe and was introduced to Britain in the 16th century. The heartwood is deep brown in colour and was highly prized for making decorative items. It was often used as a substitute for the dark wood of the tropical ebony tree. All parts of the tree are poisonous, especially the seeds.

FACT FILE

Scientific name
Laburnum anagyroides

Height 6–9 m

Where Widespread; parks, gardens

Flowering May/June

Fruiting September/October

Each hanging cluster of flowers is called a raceme

Long spikes covered in many yellow flowers

Seed pods release black seeds that are very poisonous

Seed pods (fruit) dry and open while still on the tree

Each leaflet is oval

Grey-green, with soft hairs when young

Each leaf is made up of three leaflets

ROWAN

The magical rowan tree has a past steeped in history and mythology. 'Rowan' comes from the old Norse word for tree – *raun*. Its wood was used by Druids to make their staffs and magic wands. People used to put rowan sprigs in their houses to protect them from lightning, and sailors took it on board boats to ensure safe journeys. Raw berries are poisonous, but once cooked they can be eaten.

FACT FILE

Scientific name
Sorbus aucuparia
Height 8–15 m
Where Widespread; mountains, parks, gardens
Flowering May
Fruiting October/November

The berries were once used in herbal medicines.

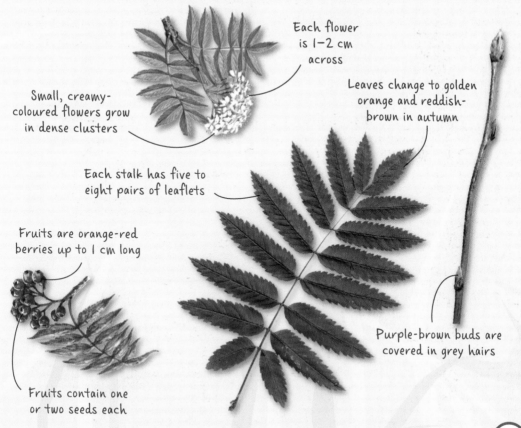

Small, creamy-coloured flowers grow in dense clusters

Each flower is 1–2 cm across

Leaves change to golden orange and reddish-brown in autumn

Each stalk has five to eight pairs of leaflets

Fruits are orange-red berries up to 1 cm long

Purple-brown buds are covered in grey hairs

Fruits contain one or two seeds each

Compound • TREES & SHRUBS 363

WALNUT

Walnut trees have been grown in Britain for their nuts, but also for their timber, which is one of the most beautiful woods in the world. There is evidence that walnuts have been growing in Britain since at least Roman times, and they were widely planted in the 1800s. Thousands of walnut trees were felled in the Napoleonic wars so that the timber could be used to make guns for soldiers.

FACT FILE

Scientific name *Juglans regia*
Height 10–30 m
Where Southern England; woodland, parks
Flowering April–June
Fruiting September/October

Male catkins (flowers) grow up to 15 cm long

Female flowers are small and green

Hollow inside

Thick with a leathery surface

Fruits are round and green

An edible nut is inside the tough outer casing

Five to nine leaflets

CEDAR OF LEBANON

This cedar is native to the mountain forests of the eastern Mediterranean, and has been a popular tree in parkland and large gardens in the UK. In ancient times, many of the cedar forests in Lebanon were felled for timber. Some stories tell of how this tree was first brought to Europe in the 18th century by a Frenchman, who uprooted a seedling while travelling in the Middle East. He stored the young tree in his hat, looking after it until his return to Paris.

FACT FILE

Scientific name *Cedrus libani*

Height 8–35 m

Where Widespread; parks, large gardens, churchyards

Flowering June–September

Fruiting August–October

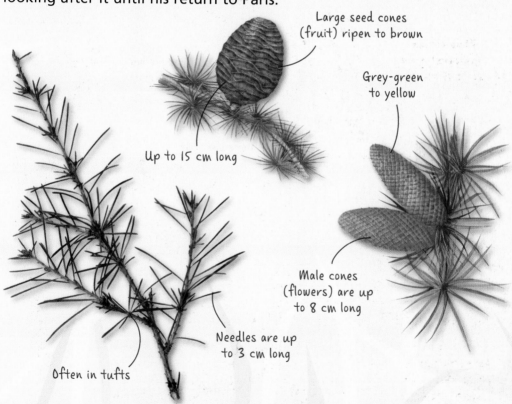

Large seed cones (fruit) ripen to brown

Up to 15 cm long

Grey-green to yellow

Male cones (flowers) are up to 8 cm long

Needles are up to 3 cm long

Often in tufts

EUROPEAN LARCH

Larches grow tall and straight and, unusually for conifers, they lose their leaves in the autumn. These fast-growing trees produce good quality timber and they are often seen growing in plantations. In Siberia, it was once believed that man was created from a larch tree, and that woman was created separately from a conifer or fir tree. Herbalists use a weak tea made from the inner bark to treat stomach upsets and asthma.

FACT FILE

Scientific name *larix decidua*
Height 12–30 m
Where Widespread; woodland, parks, gardens
Flowering March/April
Fruiting September

Seed cones (fruit) open to release seeds

Needles grow in bunches

Reddish-brown bark

Young needles

Male flowers are soft, yellow cones

Up to 3 cm long

Female flower is pink-red

GIANT SEQUOIA

The giant sequoia is one of the tallest growing plants in the world and is also one of the longest living, capable of surviving up to 4000 years. The tallest specimen is the General Sherman in the United States, which, in 1987, measured 83.8 m tall. Giant sequoias come from California and were brought to Britain in 1853, the year that the Duke of Wellington died. This is how the tree got its other name – Wellingtonia.

FACT FILE

Scientific name
Sequioadendron giganteum
Height 20–50 m
Where Widespread; parks, grounds of historic buildings
Flowering May/June
Fruiting All year

Small, cone-like male flowers

Yellow in colour and up to 1.5 cm long

Young seed cones (fruit) are green, maturing to brown

Scale-like leaves

Scales are pointed and overlapping

Up to 8 cm long

JUNIPER

Juniper is a small, slow-growing, evergreen tree and can be found in a wide range of habitats all around the world. Its fruits can take two to three years to ripen, so black and green berries can be on the same tree. These are actually soft cones rather than true berries. As birds eat them and fly to other trees, they help distribute the seeds. In folklore, in parts of southwest England, the wood and needles were burned near a sick person and this was thought to cure infection.

FACT FILE

Scientific name
Juniperus communis
Height 5–10 m
Where Southern England; woodland, scrubland, chalky soils
Flowering May/June
Fruiting All year

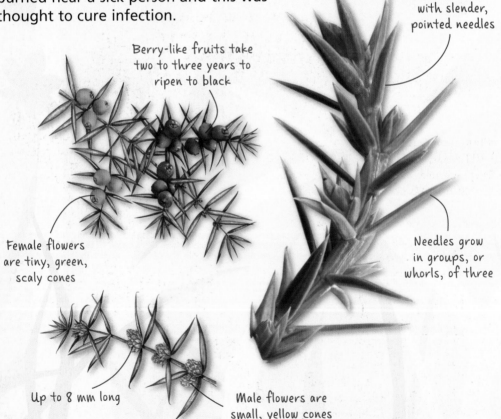

Berry-like fruits take two to three years to ripen to black

Shoots are covered with slender, pointed needles

Female flowers are tiny, green, scaly cones

Needles grow in groups, or whorls, of three

Up to 8 mm long

Male flowers are small, yellow cones

NORWAY SPRUCE

It is believed that the Norway spruce was growing in Britain long before the last Ice Age. This species did not return to Britain until around the 1500s when it was brought over from Europe. It is grown in plantations for timber and also for use as Christmas trees. The German tradition of decorating Christmas trees became fashionable in England in the 19th century after Queen Victoria married the German nobleman, Prince Albert.

FACT FILE

Scientific name *Picea abies*

Height 18–40 m

Where Widespread; plantations, parks

Flowering May

Fruiting September–November

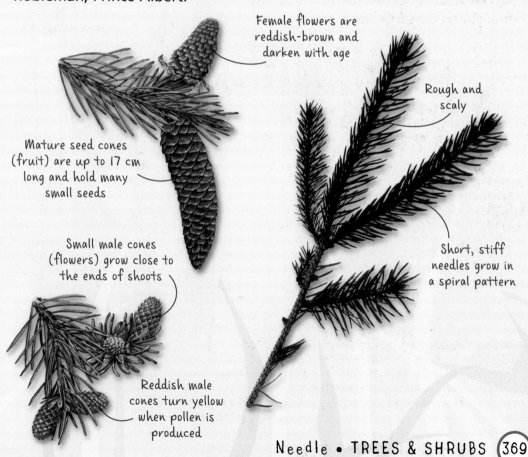

Female flowers are reddish-brown and darken with age

Rough and scaly

Mature seed cones (fruit) are up to 17 cm long and hold many small seeds

Small male cones (flowers) grow close to the ends of shoots

Short, stiff needles grow in a spiral pattern

Reddish male cones turn yellow when pollen is produced

Needle • TREES & SHRUBS 369

SCOTS PINE

There are many conifers growing in Britain today, but the Scots pine is native to parts of Scotland, making it the only native British pine. These fast-growing trees are found from Spain to Siberia. Scots pines grow tall and straight, and the wood is very hard-wearing, which makes it ideal for use as telegraph poles. The cones have been used to forecast weather – it is thought that when the cones open the air is dry, so no rain should be expected.

FACT FILE

Scientific name *Pinus sylvestris*

Height 12–36 m

Where Widespread; woodland, plantation

Flowering April

Fruiting April

Seed cones (fruit) are green at first, taking two years to ripen

Red female flowers grown in pairs

Long, slender needles up to 8 cm long

Mature seed cones are woody and up to 7 cm long

Needles grow in pairs

Small, yellow male cones (flowers) grow in groups

The dark, mysterious yew tree has been the subject of myths and legends for centuries, and it can often be found in cemeteries and church grounds. Known to live for hundreds – sometimes thousands – of years, several churchyard yews are more than 1000 years old. In ancient times, people planted yews where they would be buried. Most parts of a yew tree are extremely poisonous to humans and animals.

FACT FILE

Scientific name *Taxus baccata*
Height 4–20 m
Where Widespread; churchyards, woodland
Flowering March/April
Fruiting October

Red, berry-like fruits, called arils

Female flowers are tiny, green cones 1–2 mm long

Small male flowers turn yellow when they release pollen

Male flowers sit at the bases of leaves

Needle-like leaves

Narrow, flat and dark green

GLOSSARY

ABDOMEN The rear part of an insect's body, which usually appears segmented.

AMPHIBIAN An animal, such as a frog, that can live on both land and in water.

ANTENNAE A pair of long, sensitive feelers on an insect's head.

ARACHNID An animal, such as a spider, that has eight eggs and a body with two parts.

BIENNIAL A plant with a two-year life cycle. It takes two years to grow from a seed, produce its own seed and then die.

BIRD An animal with wings and feathers, and can usually fly.

BRACT A leaf-like part of a plant, found underneath a flower or its stalk.

BREED To mate, in order to have young.

BROADLEAF A tree with broad leaves rather than needles.

BUD A rounded, undeveloped leaf or flower, often at the end of a twig or shoot.

BUSH One plant with several woody branches, or a group of shrubs.

CAMOUFLAGE The natural colouring of an animal that enables it to blend in with its environment.

CARNIVORE An animal that feeds on meat.

CARRION Rotting animal bodies that are eaten by other animals and birds.

CATKIN A long, often hanging cluster of tiny flowers, on trees such as willows, oaks and birches.

CLUTCH A small group of eggs, laid by a bird at one time.

COLONY A large number of animals that live together in an organized group.

COMPOUND LEAF A leaf made up of several smaller leaves called leaflets.

COPPICE To cut back the stems of a tree to near ground level, causing many long, new shoots to grow up. The many straight stems that grow have traditionally been used for firewood, tools and other purposes.

CROWN The spreading branches and leaves of a tree.

CRUSTACEAN An animal, such as a crab, that has a hard shell and several pairs of legs.

CULTIVATE To grow specially.

DECIDUOUS Woody plants and trees that shed their leaves each year during autumn, with new leaves growing in spring.

ECHOLOCATION A system used by animals, such as bats and dolphins, to locate objects by bouncing sound off them.

ELYTRA The hard outer wings of a beetle.

EVERGREEN Plants and trees that keep their leaves all year round.

EXTINCTION When a plant or animal species has died out and doesn't exist anymore.

FLOCK A group of birds.

FLOWER A colourful plant, or part of a plant, that produces fruit or seeds.

FOLIAGE The leaves of a plant.

FRUIT The hard, soft or fleshy covering of the seed of flowering plants and trees.

GAPE The part of a bird's beak that opens.

GERMINATE To start to grow.

GIRTH The measurement around something, such as a tree trunk.

HABITAT An animal's or plant's natural home.

HATCH When a young animal, such as a bird, breaks out of its egg.

HEATHLAND An uncultivated area, with sandy soil and low shrubs such as heather.

HERBIVORE An animal that feeds on plants.

HIBERNATE To spend the winter in a deep sleep.

HUSK A thin, dry outer covering on fruits and seeds.

HYBRID The offspring of two similar species of animals or plants.

INSECTIVORE An animal that eats insects.

INVERTEBRATE An animal without a backbone.

JUVENILE A young animal.

LARVAE Insects that have emerged from their eggs but have not yet become adults (for example, caterpillars).

LEAFLET A leaf or leaf-like section of a compound leaf.

LOBE A rounded part of a leaf that sticks out.

MAMMAL A warm-blooded animal, covered in hair or fur, that feeds its young with milk.

MIGRATE To travel to another part of the world each year, usually by season.

MOLLUSC A type of animal that has a soft body covered by a hard shell.

MOULT To lose feathers, hair or fur, usually during warm seasons.

NATIVE Animals and plants that occur naturally in the UK and haven't been brought here by people.

NECTAR The sweet liquid produced by flowers.

NEST A place where animals shelter or live.

NOCTURNAL Animals that are active at night.

OFFSPRING An animal's young.

OMNIVORE An animal that eats both plants and meat.

OVERWINTER To remain alive through winter.

PERENNIAL A plant that lives for several years.

PESTICIDE A chemical used to kill insects and small mammals that destroy crops.

PETAL The coloured part of a flower.

PLUMAGE The feathers covering a bird's body.

POLLEN Powdery, yellow grains produced by flowering plants. It is carried by the wind or insects to other plants, enabling them to produce seeds.

POLLARD To cut back the top branches of a tree to encourage more to grow.

PREDATOR An animal that hunts, catches and kills other animals (their prey).

PREY Any animal that is hunted and then eaten by other animals.

PUPATE The process where a butterfly larva becomes a pupa.

RED LIST A list of threatened animal and plant species, put together and monitored by the IUCN.

REPTILE An animal, such as a snake, that lays eggs on land.

ROOST When animals, such as birds and bats, rest or sleep, or the name for a place where this happens.

ROOT The part of a plant or tree that grows underground and collects water and nutrients from the soil.

SCAVENGE To eat anything that can be found.

SCRUB Low-growing vegetation, often with small trees and shrubs.

SHOOT A new growth of a plant.

SHRUB A small bush with woody stems.

SPECIES A group of animals or plants that are of the same kind and are able to breed together.

STEM The long, thin part of a plant, from which leaves, flowers or fruit grow.

SUCKERS Shoots produced from the base or roots of a woody plant at a distance from the main stem.

TERRITORY An area that an animal treats as its own and defends against others.

THORAX The middle section of an insect's body, where the wings (if there are any) and legs are attached.

TREE A tall plant that has branches and leaves.

TUBER A swollen, fleshy stem or root of a plant that is usually underground and used for food storage.

TUNDRA Large, flat areas of land where it is very cold and no trees grow.

UNDERSTOREY In a wood, a layer of small trees and shrubs beneath the trees.

VEGETATION The plant life of an area.

VENOMOUS Poisonous; some snakes are venomous.

VERTEBRATE An animal with a backbone.

WINGSPAN The length from the tip of one wing to the tip of the other wing.

INDEX

Wildlife Watch is the junior branch of The Wildlife Trusts and is the UK's leading environmental action club for kids. If you care about nature and the environment and want to explore your local wildlife – this is the club for YOU!

There are 150,000 Wildlife Watch members around the UK and hundreds of local Watch groups where young people get stuck into environmental activities. Taking part in Wildlife Watch is an exciting way to explore your surroundings and get closer to the wildlife you share them with.

www.wildlifewatch.org.uk

Wildlife Watch members receive loads of exciting wildlife goodies throughout the year, including a starter pack and four issues of Wildlife Watch magazine a year. This is packed full of amazing pictures, puzzles and competitions, and a fantastic free wildlife poster comes with each issue. There's also the chance to get access to local activities and events.

Plus the fantastic website, www.wildlifewatch.org.uk, and monthly e-newsletter are packed with information. And by joining Wildlife Watch, you'll be helping your local Wildlife Trust to care for the wildlife where you live! Isn't that great?

For details on how to join, go to www.wildlifewatch.org.uk/membership or call 01636 677711.